OXFORD
UNIVERSITY PRESS

Blackstone's Police Investigators' Mock Examination Paper 2025

Pack 1

9780198935995
AF713870

Contents

OXFORD
UNIVERSITY PRESS

Great Clarendon Street, Oxford, OX2 6DP,
United Kingdom

Oxford University Press is a department of the University of Oxford.
It furthers the University's objective of excellence in research, scholarship,
and education by publishing worldwide. Oxford is a registered trade mark of
Oxford University Press in the UK and in certain other countries

First Edition published in 2004
Twenty-first Edition published in 2024

Published in the United States of America by Oxford University Press
198 Madison Avenue, New York, NY 10016, United States of America

British Library Cataloguing in Publication Data
Data available

Library of Congress Control Number
Data available

ISBN 978–0–19–893599–5

Printed in the UK by
Bell & Bain Ltd., Glasgow

MIX
Paper | Supporting responsible forestry
FSC® C007785

Acknowledgements

Thanks to all the staff at Oxford University Press, particularly Fiona Briden and Jordan Burke.

Paul Connor

Introduction to the Mock Examination

Some students taking the National Investigators' Examination (NIE) have never sat an examination of this type—some may have had the experience of taking the Sergeants' and/or Inspectors' promotion examination. Regardless of the position a student is in, preparation for the NIE can be challenging as it involves having to study a significant amount of text often in a short time frame (14 weeks or less); this is far more intense than either the Sergeants' or Inspectors' examinations.

To assist your preparation, you can obtain multiple-choice questions (MCQs) from a variety of different sources. The Blackstone's online MCQ database is an excellent resource and is available via Oxford University Press. It contains a large database of multiple-choice questions, based directly on the content of the *Blackstone's Police Investigators' Manual*, and you can find more information here: http://www.blackstonespoliceservice.com/. The *Blackstone's Police Investigators' Q&A* is also available and contains in excess of 400 questions specifically designed for the NIE student. But whilst these are helpful and assist in testing your knowledge, taking a mock examination is a different type of experience. Whilst it is impossible to recreate the exact same environment and MCQs you will face in the exam, taking this mock is a useful exercise—for example:

- It might highlight an issue with time management.
- Answering 80 MCQs is not a routine experience—simply completing the mock helps your preparation.
- It may identify strengths/weaknesses in your knowledge.

To make this mock experience as realistic as possible, it will follow the structure of an 'average' NIE as closely as possible. The first point to make here is that the examination contains 80 MCQs, 10 of which will not count towards your overall mark. These 10 MCQs are those that perform poorly against a broad range of criteria (*the sole criteria* these questions are judged against *is not* how many candidates answer the MCQ incorrectly). As analysing future candidate performance in relation to the 80 MCQs in this mock to obtain such data is not possible, 10 MCQs have been randomly selected to count as those 'poor performing' MCQs to ensure that you are marked out of 70.

The content of the MCQs in your examination is based solely on the content of the *Blackstone's Investigators' Manual 2025* and the four sections it contains (General Principles, Police Powers and Procedures; Serious Crime and Other Offences; Property Offences; and Sexual Offences) so the content of other resources has zero relevance to this mock exam.

An analysis of the structure of examinations held since March 2022 shows that the 'average' 80-question NIE consists of 35 MCQs on General Principles, Police Powers and Procedures,

19 MCQs on Serious Crime and Other Offences, 12 MCQs on Property Offences and 14 on Sexual Offences—so this mock will mirror that structure (including the 10 random MCQs that, for marking purposes, will be considered as 'poor performing' MCQs).

The presentation of MCQs in your exam follows the order of the four parts of the Manual (although not in chapter order). Mirroring that exam structure means that you will begin this mock by answering 35 randomly ordered MCQs on General Principles, Police Powers and Procedures followed by 19 randomly ordered MCQs on Serious Crime and Other Offences etc.

There can be no guarantee that this will represent the precise structure of your NIE in terms of content but the mock exam does draw from almost every chapter in the Manual at some stage so it will provide you with an opportunity to test yourself against the broad spectrum of the syllabus.

Since September 2020, the College of Policing has reserved the right to change the pass mark in the NIE *if* there is a significant variance in the pass rate of exams that are taken 'online' compared to the previous format (on paper). After each exam, the debrief panel will consider whether it is appropriate to change the exam pass mark to ensure assessment standards are in line with previous years. To date, this has not happened and, as this is a factor that is entirely out of your control, it would be sensible to set your target at 55.71% (a 'pass') but the better your score, the more likely you will be successful even if the College does consider it appropriate to raise the pass mark (it is also possible that the mark could be lowered, of course). To score 55.71%, you will need to answer 39 out of 70 questions correctly (each correct answer is worth 1.42%).

I wish you all the very best in this mock examination.

Paul Connor

Instructions for Completion

READ THE WHOLE OF THE INSTRUCTIONS BEFORE ATTEMPTING THE MOCK EXAMINATION

If you want to get the most from this mock examination, then you must treat it as if you were sitting the examination proper.

Time

You have up to two hours to complete the examination. It might not take you that long but it is best to assume that it will, so please make absolutely sure that you set aside two hours. You cannot expect to sit part of the examination for one hour, take a break for 20 minutes, return to the examination and then get an accurate picture of your performance—the examination must be completed in one two-hour sitting. However, if you have been allocated extra time to take the exam (for example, you may have been provided with reasonable adjustments because you are dyslexic), add that time to the standard two-hour exam time frame and if you include breaks, take them—the idea is that the mock exam is taken in the same circumstances as you would take the exam proper.

Environment

You need to be able to concentrate on the examination and you cannot do that if the television is on, the phone is ringing etc. Find a place where you will not be disturbed for the duration of this examination and make sure that there are no distractions that will affect your performance.

Make sure that you can see a clock, stopwatch or wristwatch.

You will need two pencils, a pencil sharpener and an eraser.

If you require any other materials in relation to reasonable adjustments, ensure they are available to you.

Pack 1

In Pack 1, you will find a blank answer sheet and the question booklet.

When you decide to start the examination, please open the question booklet. Work through the mock questions and make your choice of A, B, C or D by putting a horizontal line through the corresponding letter on the answer sheet.

Mark only one answer for each question.

Make sure that if you change your answer you erase the previous mark fully.

Pack 2

When you have finished the examination, open Pack 2 and begin the marking process. When you have finished marking your paper, please refer to the answer booklet for a detailed explanation of the correct answers with paragraph references to the *Blackstone's Police Investigators' Manual 2025*.

The marking process will take some time—to ensure accuracy; please do not rush this stage!

OXFORD
UNIVERSITY PRESS

Blackstone's Police Investigators' Mock Examination Paper 2025

Answer Sheet

1	A B C D	**31**	A B C D	**61**	A B C D
2	A B C D	**32**	A B C D	**62**	A B C D
3	A B C D	**33**	A B C D	**63**	A B C D
4	A B C D	**34**	A B C D	**64**	A B C D
5	A B C D	**35**	A B C D	**65**	A B C D
6	A B C D	**36**	A B C D	**66**	A B C D
7	A B C D	**37**	A B C D	**67**	A B C D
8	A B C D	**38**	A B C D	**68**	A B C D
9	A B C D	**39**	A B C D	**69**	A B C D
10	A B C D	**40**	A B C D	**70**	A B C D
11	A B C D	**41**	A B C D	**71**	A B C D
12	A B C D	**42**	A B C D	**72**	A B C D
13	A B C D	**43**	A B C D	**73**	A B C D
14	A B C D	**44**	A B C D	**74**	A B C D
15	A B C D	**45**	A B C D	**75**	A B C D
16	A B C D	**46**	A B C D	**76**	A B C D
17	A B C D	**47**	A B C D	**77**	A B C D
18	A B C D	**48**	A B C D	**78**	A B C D
19	A B C D	**49**	A B C D	**79**	A B C D
20	A B C D	**50**	A B C D	**80**	A B C D
21	A B C D	**51**	A B C D		
22	A B C D	**52**	A B C D		
23	A B C D	**53**	A B C D		
24	A B C D	**54**	A B C D		
25	A B C D	**55**	A B C D		
26	A B C D	**56**	A B C D		
27	A B C D	**57**	A B C D		
28	A B C D	**58**	A B C D		
29	A B C D	**59**	A B C D		
30	A B C D	**60**	A B C D		

Marking instructions

- Mark like this ~~A~~
- Make no stray marks
- Please do **NOT** tick, cross or circle

OXFORD
UNIVERSITY PRESS

Blackstone's Police Investigators' Mock Examination Paper 2025

Question Booklet

Time Allowed—120 minutes

1. Each of the questions is followed by four possible answers, only ONE of which is correct. Choose the ONE response that you consider to be correct. On the answer sheet, mark the box that corresponds to your selection. Mark your answer clearly with a — mark. The answer sheet has spaces for your answers to all questions. If you change your mind about an answer, rub out the first mark, then mark your new answer. Mark only one answer for each question.
2. You are reminded that there is no need to read the whole examination paper before beginning to select answers to the questions posed.
3. You must ensure that BEFORE the close of the examination all of your answers to the questions have been correctly entered on the answer sheet. If you leave a question unanswered for any reason, it will not receive a mark..
4. You may make any notes you wish on the question papers.

1. BUCHANAN is an extremely violent criminal who is part of a gang distributing drugs. BUCHANAN is arrested for firearms offences and is in police custody at a designated police station and will be interviewed about the offences (visual recording with sound). One of the interviewing officers, DC GRANT-MURRAY, has expert knowledge of the activities of the gang and for that reason the officer in charge of the investigation into the activities of the gang wants DC GRANT-MURRAY to interview BUCHANAN. DC GRANT-MURRAY tells the officer in charge of the case that he reasonably believes that providing his name during the course of the interview would put him in danger.

   Considering the guidance provided by Codes E and F of the Codes of Practice on such matters, which of the following comments is correct?

   A The interview should take place as normal but DC GRANT-MURRAY should only provide his warrant number (instead of his name).
   B A screen can be provided so that DC GRANT-MURRAY cannot be seen by BUCHANAN during the course of the interview.
   C If an officer of the rank of at least inspector certifies that it is necessary for the officer's safety, DC GRANT-MURRAY should give his warrant number (instead of his name) and also state the police station to which he is attached.
   D DC GRANT-MURRAY can take part in the interview but should have his back to the camera and give his warrant number (not his name) and the name of the police station to which he is attached.

2. PC OMAR is on attachment to the Criminal Investigation Department at his station and is investigating an offence of stalking (contrary to s. 2A of the Protection from Harassment Act 1997). The officer has information that causes him to suspect that COLEMAN (aged 19 years) is responsible for committing the offence. PC OMAR has tried to locate COLEMAN but has been unsuccessful and approaches DC HUTTON for some advice relating to the issuing of a warrant for the arrest of COLEMAN.

   In relation to the issuing of a warrant of arrest (under s. 125 of the Magistrates' Courts Act 1980), which of the following statements is correct?

   A A warrant cannot be issued as COLEMAN is under 21 years of age.
   B A warrant cannot be issued for COLEMAN's arrest as the offence is a summary only offence.
   C A warrant can be issued for COLEMAN's arrest; it will remain in force until it is executed, withdrawn or ceases to have effect in accordance with the rules of court.
   D A warrant can be issued for COLEMAN's arrest; the warrant has a three-month duration limit which begins on the date on which it is issued.

3. Paul and Daisy RIGBY have been married for 20 years but Paul has asked for a divorce telling Daisy he no longer loves her. When Paul asks for the divorce, Daisy loses control of her emotions and carries out a s. 47 assault (contrary to the Offences Against the Person Act 1861) against Paul. The police attend the incident leading to Daisy's arrest. Daisy is later charged with the offence and has pleaded 'not guilty' and will be conducting her own defence at the trial which will include asking questions of Paul in cross-examination.

   Can Daisy RIGBY be prevented from cross-examining Paul RIGBY in person during the trial?

   A Yes, a direction under s. 36 of the Youth Justice and Criminal Evidence Act 1999 could be given to prohibit Daisy cross-examining Paul.
   B No, Paul RIGBY is not a 'child' witness (a person under the age of 18 years).
   C Yes, Paul RIGBY would be classed as a 'protected witness'.
   D No, Daisy RIGBY has not been accused of an offence under part 1 of the Sexual Offences Act 2003.

4. PC TREACY is sent to a house which has been converted into four flats. The landlord of the house (RICHARDSON) is at the house and is complaining that one of the residents of the flats in the house (WATERFIELD) has committed an offence of theft of property from the communal kitchen area of the house and that the stolen property is in WATERFIELD's flat. RICHARDSON tells the officer that WATERFIELD is definitely not in the flat as he saw him leave the house for work around 30 minutes before the police were contacted about the theft.

   PC TREACY wants to enter the flat and search it for stolen property—what action should the officer take?

   A Obtain permission to enter and search the flat from the landlord.
   B Enter and search the flat using the power under s. 17 of the Police and Criminal Evidence Act 1984.
   C Obtain a search warrant to search for the stolen property.
   D Enter and search the flat using the power under s. 19 of the Police and Criminal Evidence Act 1984.

5. ALDRIDGE was in prison on remand for a series of robberies but was mistakenly released by prison staff. The police are urgently trying to track down ALDRIDGE's whereabouts and DC ROBINSON is part of the enquiry team. The officer receives good quality information that ALDRIDGE may seek shelter at a garage owned by WOODWARD and the officer wants to set up directed surveillance on the premises as a matter of urgency.

   Which of the following comments is correct in relation to authorising directed surveillance?

   A An authorisation for directed surveillance must be sought from an officer of the rank of superintendent or above who can authorise (in writing only) urgent directed surveillance for a period not exceeding 72 hours.
   B An authorisation for directed surveillance must be sought from an officer of the rank of superintendent or above who can authorise (in writing or orally) urgent directed surveillance for a period not exceeding 96 hours.
   C An authorisation for directed surveillance could be sought from an officer of the rank of inspector who can authorise (in writing only) urgent directed surveillance for a period not exceeding 72 hours.
   D An authorisation for directed surveillance could be sought from an officer of the rank of inspector who can authorise (in writing or orally) urgent directed surveillance for a period not exceeding 96 hours.

6. ARMSTRONG is attacked and robbed by MYATT (who is a stranger to ARMSTRONG). DC WESTON is first to arrive at the scene of the offence and quickly obtains a first description of MYATT from ARMSTRONG. DC WESTON places ARMSTRONG in an unmarked police vehicle and drives ARMSTRONG around the local area to see if he can identify the person responsible for the offence. They drive along a busy street with a cafe on one side of the road and a pub on the other. People are outside both premises and ARMSTRONG is looking intently at a group outside the cafe. DC WESTON sees a person who matches the description given by ARMSTRONG standing outside the pub with a group of people and asks ARMSTRONG to look closely at the group outside the pub. As a result, ARMSTRONG identifies MYATT who is in the group outside the pub and is subsequently arrested by other officers searching the area.

   In relation to Code D of the Codes of Practice, which of the following comments is correct?

   A Code D has not been complied with as once a first description of an offender has been obtained from an eyewitness they should not take part in any 'street' identification process.
   B Code D has not been complied with as DC WESTON is not allowed to draw the attention of ARMSTRONG to a particular group.
   C Code D has not been complied with as at least two officers must be present when such a 'street' identification process takes place.
   D Code D of the Codes of Practice has been complied with by the officer.

7. FIELDING has been arrested for drug-related crimes. At the custody block, the arresting officer informs the custody sergeant that there is evidence that FIELDING has swallowed some drugs. FIELDING's detention is authorised and the officers wish to carry out an X-ray or ultrasound scan on FIELDING.

   In order to comply with s. 55A of PACE 1984, which of the following statements is correct?

   A The drug swallowed must be a Class A and have been for supply or export. The authority required is that of an inspector and force can be used.
   B The drug swallowed must be a Class A drug and have been for supply or export. The authority required is that of an inspector (along with the consent of FIELDING) and no force can be used.
   C The drug swallowed can be a Class A, B or C and have been for supply or export. The authority required is that of an inspector (along with the consent of FIELDING) and no force can be used.
   D The drug swallowed can be a Class A, B or C and have been for supply or export. The authority required is that of an inspector and force can be used.

8. SAVELIO is a member of a gang which is responsible for a series of robberies. SAVELIO is arrested at the scene of the gang's latest robbery but the other members of the gang manage to escape. SAVELIO is taken to a designated police station where he requests that his friend, McLEAN, is informed of his arrest. The arresting officer, DC BECK, believes that McLEAN is the person who handles the stolen goods from the robberies and that informing McLEAN of SAVELIO's arrest will hinder the recovery of property from the robberies. DC BECK wishes to delay SAVELIO's exercise of this right.

   Which of the statements below is correct?

   A The delay can be authorised by an inspector. The maximum period of the delay is 36 hours.
   B The delay can be authorised by an inspector. The maximum period of the delay is 48 hours.
   C The delay must be authorised by a superintendent. The maximum period of the delay is 36 hours.
   D The delay must be authorised by a superintendent. The maximum period of the delay is 48 hours.

9. HUSSAIN has attended a designated police station voluntarily to be interviewed regarding an offence of assault. HUSSAIN arrived at the police station at 13.30 hours and was arrested for the offence at 14.00 hours. He has been interviewed about the offence and began an eight-hour rest period at 22.00 hours. At 23.30 hours, HUSSAIN's solicitor requested a consultation with him which was allowed to take place by the custody officer, PS MILLS.

In relation to HUSSAIN's eight-hour rest period, which of the following comments is correct?

A HUSSAIN's rest period should not have been interrupted at the request of his legal representative.
B A fresh eight-hour period for rest is not required once the consultation is concluded.
C In any period of 24 hours, a detainee must be allowed a continuous period of at least eight hours for rest—in HUSSAIN's case, the period of 24 hours runs from the time of his arrival at the police station.
D HUSSAIN's rest period can only be interrupted where there are reasonable grounds for believing that not interrupting it would involve a risk of harm to people or serious loss of, or damage to, property.

10. UMPLEBY has been arrested for an offence of violent disorder and is being interviewed about the offence at a designated police station—the interview is being visually recorded. UMPLEBY is legally represented in the interview by his solicitor. The interviewing officers ask a number of questions of UMPLEBY during the interview but he remains completely silent having been told to do so by his solicitor who has told the interviewing officers that he has advised his client to do so in response to all questions put to him in interview. UMPLEBY genuinely relies on the advice of his solicitor to remain silent.

Could adverse inferences (under s. 34 of the Criminal Justice and Public Order Act 1994) be drawn from UMPLEBY's failure to respond to questions in the interview?

A No, UMPLEBY's genuine reliance on the advice of his solicitor to stay silent is not, in itself, enough to preclude adverse inferences.
B Yes, UMPLEBY could be convicted solely on an inference drawn from silence.
C No, adverse inferences can only be drawn from an interview where the defendant responds to questioning; they cannot be drawn from an interview where the defendant remains silent.
D Yes, adverse inferences may be drawn from UMPLEBY's silence but only because he was legally represented during the course of the interview.

11. DALMAN persuades KINCADE and FRASER to take part in a theft at a newsagent's shop. The agreed plan is that the three men will enter the newsagents, distract the newsagent and steal from the till. KINCADE tells DALMAN he will go along with the plan on the strict understanding violence is not going to be threatened or used and DALMAN agrees. Privately, DALMAN tells FRASER he is taking a knife with him and will use it on the newsagent if necessary; FRASER tells DALMAN that is OK as far as he is concerned. The three go to the newsagent's and carry out the theft but they are disturbed by the newsagent; FRASER encourages DALMAN to use violence on the newsagent and shouts out '*Stab him!*' DALMAN stabs the newsagent who is seriously injured as a result.

With regard to the law relating to 'parasitic accessory liability' and the wounding offence, which of the following comments is correct?

A Only DALMAN would be liable for the wounding offence.
B DALMAN and FRASER are liable for the injury to the newsagent (the prosecution only need to prove that FRASER had foresight that the wounding would occur).
C DALMAN and FRASER are liable for the injury to the newsagent (the prosecution need to prove that FRASER intended to assist or encourage the wounding offence).
D DALMAN, KINCADE and FRASER are liable for the wounding offence.

12. DEWICK is 15 years old and has been arrested for an offence of theft. The custody officer, PS WHEELER, makes contact with DEWICK's biological father who arrives at the police station 30 minutes after the contact from PS WHEELER was made. DEWICK expressly and specifically refuses to have his biological father act as an appropriate adult as he is estranged from him, the last contact between the two being over three years earlier. DEWICK's biological father is told of this but demands that he is allowed to look after his son's welfare.

What should happen in these circumstances?

A The custody officer can allow DEWICK's father to act as an appropriate adult in this situation.
B As DEWICK expressly and specifically objects to the presence of his biological father, his father should not be asked to act as the appropriate adult.
C An officer of the rank of inspector or above would have to authorise the exclusion of DEWICK's biological father.
D DEWICK's biological father must be allowed to act as the appropriate adult.

13. HARDCASTLE was arrested for an offence of robbery. Whilst in police detention, his fingerprints were taken and he was later bailed for further enquiries to be made in relation to the offence. It is subsequently discovered that the fingerprints obtained from HARDCASTLE were not of sufficient quality to allow satisfactory analysis to take place.

In relation to a requirement for HARDCASTLE to attend a police station to have his fingerprints taken, which of the following comments is correct?

A HARDCASTLE can be required to attend a police station for his fingerprints to be obtained, although no power of arrest exists should he decline to attend.

B If there is an urgent need for HARDCASTLE's fingerprints to be obtained for the purposes of the investigation of the offence, an officer of the rank of inspector or above may authorise a period shorter than seven days for HARDCASTLE to attend the police station.

C HARDCASTLE should be given a period of at least 14 days within which to attend a police station to have his fingerprints taken.

D HARDCASTLE cannot be required to attend a police station for an additional set of fingerprints to be taken unless he has been charged or reported for an offence.

14. PEGLER has been charged with an offence of attempted rape and the issue of bail is now being considered. PEGLER has a previous conviction for manslaughter, for which he served five years' imprisonment (that manslaughter conviction is 12 years old) and he has no other previous convictions.

Will the provisions of s. 25 of the Criminal Justice and Public Order Act 1994 be applicable in these circumstances?

A Yes, as PEGLER will not be granted bail unless there are exceptional circumstances which justify it.

B No, as PEGLER's previous conviction for manslaughter is over 10 years old.

C Yes, due to the nature of the charge and because of PEGLER's previous conviction, he cannot be granted bail.

D No, as s. 25 only relates to defendants charged with murder, attempted murder or manslaughter.

15. A large number of burglaries at commercial premises have taken place and goods to the value of £2 million pounds have been stolen. An operation is commenced in relation to the offences leading to the arrest of RUSSELL who is later charged with the burglary offences. Sergeant EDWARDS is the disclosure officer in the case and is liaising with his Professional Standards Department as to whether information regarding allegations of, and the misconduct of, several officers involved in the investigation should be revealed to the prosecutor.

Considering the Disclosure Code of Practice and advice given to prosecutors by the DPP, which of the following comments is correct?

A Sergeant EDWARDS will have the final responsibility for the value judgement on whether information relating to misconduct of police officers should be revealed to the prosecutor.
B Findings in relation to disciplinary matters, regardless of their nature, must always be revealed to the prosecution which must, in turn, disclose them to the defence.
C There is no duty on the prosecution to disclose details of unsubstantiated complaints against a police officer.
D Disciplinary matters are not criminal convictions and consequently have no relevance as far as disclosure is concerned.

16. RUBIO has been arrested in connection with an offence of attempted kidnapping. The victim states that when RUBIO tried to kidnap her, he was not wearing a top of any description and she managed to scratch him on the chest with her fingernails. The victim states that the scratches were deep and left four large marks on the left side of RUBIO's chest. The officer in the case, DS PEARSON, wishes to examine RUBIO under s. 54A of the Police and Criminal Evidence Act 1984 (as amended by the Anti-terrorism, Crime and Security Act 2001), to ascertain whether or not he has such marks on his chest as their presence would tend to identify him as the person involved in the commission of the offence.

Which of the following statements is correct?

A The custody officer can authorise that RUBIO be examined without his consent but this must be authorised in writing.
B RUBIO can be examined for the presence of the marks but only if he consents and an officer of the rank of inspector or above authorises the examination.
C RUBIO cannot be examined as the Act allows only for the search and/or examination of an individual to establish their identification and not for evidence in relation to the offence for which they have been arrested.
D An inspector must authorise the examination; authorisation can be given orally or in writing.

17. PC LODGE has arrested EASTMAN in relation to an offence of robbery. The officer is putting together an interview plan which involves consideration of what information to make available to EASTMAN's solicitor, HERSON. PC LODGE approaches you, as her supervisor, for some advice regarding what should be disclosed to a solicitor prior to the interview with EASTMAN. The officer is unsure about whether the custody record and an initial description given by a witness of the offender (the 'first description') should be disclosed.

Must both or either of these items be disclosed to HERSON before the interview with EASTMAN takes place?

A Yes, the custody record and the record of 'first description' must be provided to HERSON before EASTMAN is interviewed about the offence.
B No, there is no provision within the Police and Criminal Evidence Act 1984 or the Codes of Practice for the disclosure of any information by the police at the police station.
C Yes, the custody record must be disclosed.
D No, although if these items are not disclosed then no inference could be drawn by a court from EASTMAN's silence.

18. BAKER has attended a designated police station at the request of PC ISHAQ to take part in a voluntary interview regarding an allegation of theft. It is PC ISHAQ's intention that the interview will be audio recorded but when BAKER arrives at the police station, the two interview rooms at the police station are unavailable (one of the rooms has a fault with the recording equipment and the other is being used to interview a suspect and will not be available for some time).

If a written record of the interview is to be made, who would be the 'relevant officer' in these circumstances?

A An officer of the rank of inspector or above.
B The custody officer at the designated police station.
C PC ISHAQ (the interviewing officer).
D An officer of the rank of sergeant or above.

19. GILBERT (aged 16 years) has been arrested for an offence of robbery (a recordable offence) and has been transported to the custody block of a designated police station. DC JACKMAN (the officer in the case) interviews GILBERT in the presence of O'TOOLE (who is GILBERT's uncle and acting as an appropriate adult). During the interview, DC JACKMAN tells GILBERT that he wishes to obtain footwear impressions from him (under s. 61A of the Police and Criminal Evidence Act 1984) and asks for his consent—GILBERT refuses.

Can DC JACKMAN obtain footwear samples from GILBERT in these circumstances?

A No, as footwear samples can only be obtained from a person in police detention with their written consent.
B Yes, and DC JACKMAN can use force to obtain them if necessary.
C No, unless O'TOOLE provides written consent for DC JACKMAN to obtain footwear impressions from GILBERT.
D Yes, if the impressions are necessary to prove or disprove GILBERT's involvement in the robbery offence.

20. WEBBER had a short relationship with ASHCROFT but ASHCROFT broke up with WEBBER. WEBBER wants revenge against ASHCROFT and wishes to cause him problems but is scared of doing anything herself, so she encourages MARTIN to cause criminal damage to a VW Golf car owned by ASHCROFT. MARTIN agrees and visits ASHCROFT's house. He sees a VW Golf outside ASHCROFT's house and slashes all the tyres with a knife but he has made a mistake as the car does not belong to ASHCROFT—it belongs to GOODEY. GOODEY sees MARTIN damaging his car and confronts MARTIN. In the struggle that follows, MARTIN commits a s. 39 battery offence (contrary to the Criminal Justice Act 1988) against GOODEY.

In relation to the criminal damage and the battery, would the doctrine of transferred *mens rea* apply to WEBBER in these circumstances?

A Yes, but WEBBER would only be liable as an accessory to the criminal damage to GOODEY's car.
B No, the doctrine has no applicability in this situation as it is only relevant when considering offences against the person under the Offences Against the Person Act 1861.
C Yes, WEBBER is liable as an accessory to the criminal damage and s.39 battery offence.
D No, transferred *mens rea* does not apply to WEBBER as she is an accessory—the doctrine only has applicability when considerig the actions of a principal offender.

21. PC DEARLOVE is directed to attend a call where it is reported that a person is behaving suspiciously around some farm buildings. The officer arrives at the scene and sees NEDD walking out of a farm building and across a field. There is a very large sign next to the field indicating that it is private property. As NEDD climbs over a fence and into the road, PC DEARLOVE stops him. NEDD admits he was looking for somewhere to sleep for the night and was trespassing. The officer searches NEDD and finds an air pistol in his possession. PC DEARLOVE arrests NEDD in respect of his commission of an offence of trespassing with a firearm on land (contrary to s. 20(2) of the Firearms Act 1968 and using the provisions of s. 24 of the Police and Criminal Evidence Act 1984). PC DEARLOVE now wishes to use the provisions of s. 32 of the Police and Criminal Evidence Act 1984 to search NEDD and the nearby farm building.

With regard to the officer's powers under s. 32 of the Police and Criminal Evidence Act 1984, which of the following comments is true?

A PC DEARLOVE cannot search the farm building that NEDD was seen walking out from under s. 32 of the Act.
B PC DEARLOVE has a power under s. 32 to search NEDD for evidence but only for evidence specifically relating to the offence for which he was arrested.
C PC DEARLOVE may require NEDD to remove his outer coat, jacket and gloves for the purpose of the search but he cannot search in NEDD's mouth.
D If PC DEARLOVE suspects that NEDD may present a danger to himself or others, then he may search him.

22. PC SWIFT attends the scene of a theft of cash from an office block. When the officer walks into the office, she is approached by WARDLE who states, '*Officer, I stole the money. I want to confess.*' WARDLE is arrested for theft and taken to a designated police station. PC SWIFT records the comment made by WARDLE as soon as practicable, noting when it was made and signing it in her pocket book.

Which of the following comments is correct regarding the comment made by WARDLE to PC SWIFT?

A It is a 'significant statement' and it should be put to WARDLE at the beginning of the interview with him, after caution and before questioning.
B It is not a 'significant statement' as it was made at an office block rather than at a designated police station.
C It is a 'significant statement' and it should be put to WARDLE at the conclusion of any interview with him and at the end of questioning.
D It is not a 'significant statement' as it was not made in response to and after any form of caution.

23. JOSHUA has been charged with an offence of burglary and has been bailed by PS OBI (the custody officer). PS OBI imposed a number of bail conditions on JOSHUA, including a curfew between set times. One week after being bailed, JOSHUA finds out that his girlfriend is pregnant and wants to have his bail condition of curfew modified so that he can help his girlfriend during her pregnancy.

Which of the following comments is correct in respect of varying the bail condition?

A JOSHUA must speak to PS OBI who is the only person who can vary the conditions of bail.
B JOSHUA's conditions of bail can be varied by PS OBI or another custody officer serving at any police station in PS OBI's force area.
C JOSHUA's conditions of bail can be varied by PS OBI or another custody officer serving at the same police station that PS OBI works at.
D JOSHUA's conditions of bail can be varied but only by a magistrates' court.

24. GIBB (who is 18 years old) and MUTCH (who is 17 years old) have been arrested in connection with an offence of robbery. The officer in charge of the case, DC HEINZMAN, has information and evidence that GIBB and MUTCH are responsible for a large number of other robbery offences and wishes to speak to them about these offences. As such, DC HEINZMAN seeks to have GIBB and MUTCH committed to detention at a police station under s. 128 of the Magistrates' Courts Act 1980 so that he can speak to them about the other robbery offences.

Which of the following comments is correct in relation to such a remand?

A GIBB could be remanded in police custody for a period not exceeding three clear days; MUTCH could not be remanded in police custody as he is a juvenile.
B GIBB could be remanded in police custody for a period not exceeding three clear days; MUTCH could be remanded in police custody for a period not exceeding 24 hours.
C GIBB and MUTCH could be remanded in police custody for a period not exceeding three clear days.
D GIBB and MUTCH could be remanded in police custody for a period not exceeding 24 hours.

25. TOWERS contacts DC ANSLOW with information in relation to a large shipment of drugs being moved in an articulated lorry. TOWERS works in a transport depot and states that he heard several of his work colleagues talking about the shipment and that they would finalise details at a meeting at the depot in approximately four hours' time. TOWERS tells DC ANSLOW that he can provide further information about the shipment to assist the police. In order to do so, DC ANSLOW requires urgent authorisation for TOWERS to act as a Covert Human Intelligence Source (CHIS).

In relation to such an 'urgent' CHIS authorisation, which of the following comments is correct?

A An officer of at least the rank of inspector can authorise 'urgent' CHIS activity; the authorisation must be given in writing and will last for 72 hours.
B An officer of at least the rank of inspector can authorise 'urgent' CHIS activity; the authorisation can be provided orally or in writing and will last for 24 hours.
C An officer of at least the rank of superintendent must authorise 'urgent' CHIS activity; the authorisation can be given orally or in writing and will last for 48 hours.
D An officer of at least the rank of superintendent must authorise 'urgent' CHIS activity; the authorisation can be given orally or in writing and will last for 96 hours.

26. DERRY has been charged with an offence of assault (contrary to s. 47 of the Offences Against the Person Act 1861) and has been bailed by the police to make a first appearance at a magistrates' court in relation to the offence. DERRY does not appear at court on that date and is later arrested for absconding (under s. 7 of the Bail Act 1976). When arrested, DERRY states that he had a reasonable excuse for his failure to appear as he made a genuine error about his date of appearance at the magistrates' court; this came about because the police failed to give him a copy of the record of the decision to bail him (which included the date on which he was supposed to appear).

In relation to the offence under s. 6 of the Bail Act 1976 (offence of absconding by a person released on bail), which of the following comments is correct?

A DERRY has a 'reasonable excuse' for his failure to appear (the failure by the police to provide him with a copy of the record of the decision).
B The offence under s. 6 would not be appropriate as this is limited to a situation where the person fails to appear at a court having been granted bail by a court (not 'police bail').
C The facts that DERRY made a genuine error about his date of appearance and that the police did not give him a copy of the record of the bail decision are irrelevant; he has committed the offence in these circumstances.
D DERRY has a 'reasonable excuse' for his failure to appear (the fact that he made a genuine error about his date of appearance).

27. STACEY has been arrested in relation to an offence of robbery. He denies any involvement in the offence, disputing the identification evidence. STACEY has indicated that he will not take part in any video identification or identification parade so consideration is being given to a group identification process.

Considering Annex C of Code D of the Codes of Practice (dealing with group identification), which of the following statements is correct?

A A group identification may only take place with STACEY's consent and cooperation.
B A group identification process can take place at a police station.
C A group identification process must involve a moving (not stationary) group.
D A group identification process must be video recorded in all circumstances.

28. KINGSLEY and NORTH have been living together for over 20 years. The relationship is volatile and they frequently have loud and long arguments with each other resulting, on more than one occasion, in concerned neighbours contacting the police to deal with the disturbance their behaviour causes. One evening, the pair are arguing about a football match on TV when KINGSLEY loses his temper, picks up a TV remote control and throws it at NORTH (only intending to cause her minor injury). The TV remote control hits NORTH behind the ear. Unknown to anyone, NORTH has an unusual weakness of the vertebral artery and the blow with the TV remote control ruptures the artery causing her death.

Considering the law relating to the chain of causation and intervening acts, which of the following statements is correct?

A KINGSLEY is not liable for the death of NORTH as he did not intend to kill her or cause her grievous bodily harm.
B KINGSLEY is liable for the death of NORTH and the fact that the consequences of KINGSLEY's actions are much more acute (NORTH is dead rather than injured) is just KINGSLEY's bad luck.
C KINGSLEY is liable for the death of NORTH as 'but for' his actions NORTH would not be dead (this is an example of the fact that the chain of causation can never be broken regardless of the circumstances).
D KINGSLEY is not liable for the death of NORTH as no reasonable person could have ever foreseen that death would occur as a consequence of such a minor injury.

29. DC BAKER is working in the Criminal Investigation Department at his station when he receives good-quality intelligence from a trusted source in relation to the location of a large amount of stolen goods. The stolen property is alleged to be located at five different premises and, after briefly discussing the matter with his supervisor, DC BAKER decides to make an application to search all the premises (an 'all premises' warrant). Due to the nature of the intelligence received by DC BAKER, he decides to request that the warrant allow entry to the target premises on multiple occasions.

In relation to the procedures under ss. 15 and 16 of the Police and Criminal Evidence Act 1984 (application for a warrant and execution of a warrant) and Code B of the Codes of Practice, which of the following comments is correct?

A Applications for multiple premises and multiple entry warrants must be made with the written authority of an officer of at least the rank of superintendent (although in urgent cases where a superintendent is not readily available, the most senior officer on duty may authorise the application).
B Entry and search under such a warrant must be made within one month from the date of its issue.
C No premises may be entered or searched for the second or any subsequent time under a warrant which authorises multiple entries unless a police officer of at least the rank of inspector has, in writing, authorised that entry to those premises.
D If the warrant is an all premises warrant, no premises which are not specified in it may be entered and searched unless a police officer of at least the rank of superintendent has, in writing, authorised them to be entered.

30. ELVY, an adult male, has been arrested for several offences of burglary and you intend to search properties that may have evidence relating to the offences that ELVY has been arrested for. ELVY occupies a house at 22 Cross Avenue, which he rents from the estate agents Manning and Sons and he also owns and controls a lock-up garage which he uses to keep his car in. You have intelligence at your disposal which indicates that ELVY rents a storage facility in a warehouse but this is unconfirmed and you only reasonably suspect that he controls the storage facility.

With the correct authorisation from an inspector or above, which of the following statements is correct as to which properties can be searched by a constable under s. 18 of PACE 1984?

A All three properties can be searched.
B The storage facility and the house he rents.
C Only the house he rents.
D The house he rents and his garage.

31. A group of trainee investigators are taking part in an interviewing training course where tactics and techniques in relation to interviewing suspects and witnesses to offences are being discussed. A number of comments are made in relation to the mode of addressing a person being interviewed and the need to avoid language that is demeaning. This generates a discussion in relation to harassment in the workplace and the potential for the Equality Act 2010 to be breached in certain circumstances.

When considering s. 26 of the Act (in particular, sexual harassment under s. 26(2)), which of the following comments is correct?

A A man calling another man 'lad' is not demeaning.
B Referring to women as 'chicks' is not demeaning.
C Referring to women as 'babes' is not demeaning.
D Referring to a woman using the term 'sweetie' is not demeaning.

32. Lance DALLOW lives in a house with TITUS (his long-term partner of 15 years) and Brian DALLOW (his 40-year-old brother). Lance DALLOW is morbidly obese and lives in an upstairs bedroom of the house; TITUS and Brian DALLOW have voluntarily undertaken to care for Lance DALLOW as a result of his infirmity. Over a period of time, TITUS and Brian DALLOW ignore Lance DALLOW and do not take him any food or drinks resulting in Lance DALLOW dying from neglect.

Solely in relation to the law regarding omissions, which of the following statements is correct?

A TITUS and Brian DALLOW would not be liable for the death of Lance DALLOW as they did not have a statutory obligation to care for him.
B TITUS and Brian DALLOW would not be liable for the death of Lance DALLOW as neither were in a parental relationship with him.
C Brian DALLOW would be liable for the death of Lance DALLOW as he has a family relationship with Lance DALLOW; TITUS would not be liable for the death of Lance DALLOW.
D TITUS and Brian DALLOW would be liable for the death of Lance DALLOW.

33. COWLAM has been charged with murder. COWLAM's defence team have disclosed details of a witness (KHOKHAR) they propose to call as an alibi witness for the prosecution and the police officer in charge of the case, Inspector HASTINGS, proposes to conduct an interview with KHOKHAR.

In relation to the Code of Practice for Arranging and Conducting Interviews of Witnesses Notified by the Accused (under s. 21A of the Criminal Procedure and Investigations Act 1996), which of the following comments is correct?

A KHOKHAR is not entitled to be accompanied by a solicitor at the interview.
B KHOKHAR is not obliged to attend the proposed interview.
C KHOKHAR is entitled to be accompanied by a solicitor at the interview; the attendance of the solicitor will be funded by the Legal Services Commission.
D KHOKHAR must be interviewed by an officer of the rank of sergeant or above.

34. BERWICK has been arrested on suspicion of rape and has been taken to a designated police station. BERWICK is given his rights by the custody officer, PS McMILLAN, and requests that he is represented by FORD (his solicitor) whilst he is in police custody. The officer in charge of the case, DC JAMEEL, believes that FORD will act in a way that will interfere with evidence connected to the rape.

In relation to Code C and BERWICK's right to legal advice, which of the following comments is correct?

A DC JAMEEL should seek a superintendent's authority to deny BERWICK access to legal advice from FORD.
B BERWICK should be allowed to speak with FORD but, to ensure that FORD acts ethically, his consultations with BERWICK can be monitored by a police officer.
C Once the decision has been taken to deny BERWICK his legal advice, the authorisation applies to all solicitors or legal advisers and lasts up to a maximum of 36 hours.
D BERWICK cannot be denied access to legal advice from FORD in these circumstances.

35. Luke RAILTON has been arrested on suspicion of committing an offence of murder. At the time of the offence, Emma RAILTON (the wife of Luke RAILTON) was with her husband and, although she had no involvement in the offence, she did see exactly what happened. While Luke RAILTON is in custody awaiting interview, DC PAPWORTH (who is part of the investigation team) is gathering evidence and interviews Emma RAILTON about the incident. DC PAPWORTH obtains a witness statement from Emma RAILTON describing what she saw occur. Luke RAILTON is charged with the murder offence and pleads 'not guilty'.

Considering the law in respect of the compellability of Emma RAILTON to give evidence for the prosecution, which of the following statements is correct?

A The statement from Emma RAILTON could be admitted in evidence even if she refused to give evidence against her husband.
B Emma RAILTON is not compellable to give evidence against her husband in this matter and DC PAPWORTH should have informed her of this before taking any statement; the statement obtained could not be admitted in evidence.
C Murder is a 'specified offence' under s. 80(2A) of the Police and Criminal Evidence Act 1984, meaning that Emma RAILTON is compellable to give evidence for the prosecution.
D A wife cannot be compelled to give evidence against her husband regardless of the crime the husband is accused of.

36. FOX is the owner of a breakfast/burger van which he pitches in a lay-by on a busy industrial estate. FOX is doing quite well as the quality of his food is good but his success is having an impact on BRITTAIN's similar business which also operates from the industrial estate. BRITTAIN has asked FOX to leave on several occasions and believes he has the right to do so as he was the first to do business on the estate; FOX has ignored him. BRITTAIN is becoming desperate as his business is failing, so he hides an unloaded shotgun beneath his coat and visits FOX's van. FOX is not actually working in the van when BRITTAIN arrives but CHURCH (FOX's girlfriend) is. BRITTAIN tells CHURCH that FOX has one week to '*pack up and go*' or there will be consequences. When CHURCH asks what kind of consequences, BRITTAIN reveals the shotgun and says, '*I will kill your boyfriend*'. BRITTAIN has no intention of following through with his threat but does intend CHURCH to fear that he will kill FOX. In fact, CHURCH does not believe BRITTAIN at all.

Considering only the offence of threats to kill (contrary to s. 16 of the Offences Against the Person Act 1861), which of the comments below is true?

A The offence is not committed by FOX as CHURCH does not believe the threat.
B FOX commits the offence in these circumstances.
C The offence is not committed as the threat was made to a third party (CHURCH).
D The threat must be made with the intention that the person who receives it will then and there fear for their life or the life of another. As the threat was made to kill FOX in a week's time, BRITTAIN would not commit the offence.

37. HOPPER is sitting in the living room of his house with several friends—they are all watching an international rugby match between England and Scotland. It is a very hot day so he has the windows of the living room open. During the match, the Scottish team score a try causing HOPPER to scream in rage as he is supporting England. He uses extremely abusive language about the Scottish team and, in doing so, he intends to stir up racial hatred against the Scottish. As the windows in the living room are open, this abusive language is heard by SEARBY who is HOPPER's neighbour and is Scottish. SEARBY contacts the police to complain about HOPPER's language. The language was not heard by anyone else.

In relation to the offence under s. 18 of the Public Order Act 1986 (use of words, behaviour or display of written material), which of the following comments is correct?

A The offence has been committed but only in relation to SEARBY (as he was not inside the same dwelling as HOPPER).
B The offence has not been committed as it cannot be committed by a person who is inside a dwelling.
C The offence has been committed in relation to HOPPER's friends in the living room of his house and also in relation to SEARBY.
D The offence is not committed as the language used by HOPPER was not heard by anyone except for people in the same dwelling as HOPPER or in another dwelling (SEARBY).

38. RICHARDSON returns home early from work, walks into the living room of her house and discovers her husband having sexual intercourse with her best friend on the living room floor. RICHARDSON tries to keep composed and walks through the living room and out into the back garden but five minutes later she loses control because of the act of sexual infidelity. She goes back into the living room, picks up a heavy glass ornament and attacks her husband and her best friend. RICHARDSON kills her husband and seriously injures her best friend. When interviewed about the incident, RICHARDSON tells the police she lost control and intended to kill them both.

Could RICHARDSON utilise the 'special defence' of 'loss of control' if charged with the murder of her husband and the attempted murder of her best friend?

A Yes, but only in relation to a charge of murder of her husband.
B Yes, if RICHARDSON can prove that a person with a normal degree of tolerance and self-restraint and in the circumstances would have reacted in the same or a similar way.
C No, the sexual infidelity of her husband is not a loss of control 'qualifying trigger' and in relation to her best friend the charge is not one of murder.
D No, because the special defence of 'loss of control' requires the loss of control to be sudden.

39. CLARKE and TUCKER are walking towards WORSFOLD'S house. TUCKER's mobile phone rings and TUCKER has a brief conversation and hangs up. TUCKER tells CLARKE that he has to go to his mother's house and cannot accompany CLARKE to WORSFOLD's house. TUCKER passes CLARKE a small envelope and asks CLARKE to give it to WORSFOLD as WORSFOLD is expecting it. CLARKE asks what is in the envelope and TUCKER replies *'£200 cash'*. CLARKE has no reason to disbelieve TUCKER and tells him that he will deliver the money to WORSFOLD. CLARKE continues his journey and on the way to WORSFOLD's house he is stopped by a police officer. The police officer searches CLARKE and finds the envelope. When the officer opens the envelope, it is found to contain an amount of cocaine and not £200 cash as CLARKE had been informed.

Is CLARKE in 'possession' of the cocaine?

A Yes, as he has physical control over it as well as knowledge of its presence.
B No, as although he knew he had possession of the envelope, he did not know that it contained cocaine.
C Yes, as all that is required to prove 'possession' is that a person has physical control over something.
D No, as he thought there was £200 cash inside the envelope.

40. SKELTON (a British citizen) owns a house just outside Dunkirk on the coast of Northern France. He is finding the upkeep of the property hard going and is really short of cash and thinks he can make easy money by transporting refugees from France to England to be exploited as sources of cheap labour in England. SKELTON knows that there is a refugee camp a few miles from his house in France and visits it. It does not take him long to find plenty of refugees who voluntarily pay him €500 each to get to England. SKELTON arranges to transport 20 refugees in an 8-metre dinghy he owns and tells the refugees to meet him on the beach later that evening. SKELTON arrives on the beach in the dinghy later that night and the refugees get into it but, before it even moves, the engine breaks down and SKELTON has to return the money to the refugees.

Does SKELTON commit an offence of human trafficking (contrary to s. 2 of the Modern Slavery Act 2015)?

A Yes, the offence is committed as soon as SKELTON arranges the travel of the refugees with a view to them being exploited.
B No, none of the activities take place in the United Kingdom.
C Yes, but only when he tries to physically transport them (at that point they are being 'trafficked').
D No, the refugees were not 'trafficked' (they did not arrive in the United Kingdom).

41. Kurt SWINNEY and Bianca SWINNEY are the parents of Rebecca SWINNEY (who is 15 years old). Kurt and Bianca have separated, resulting in a child arrangements order being made in respect of Rebecca SWINNEY directing that she will live with her mother (Bianca) at her home which is in Workington in Cumbria. Bianca decides to take Rececca on a holiday visiting Scotland and then flying to Norway—the holiday lasts three weeks. Kurt SWINNEY only discovers that Bianca has taken Rebecca on the holiday after she returns from Norway and he complains to the police that this is an offence of child abduction by Bianca SWINNEY.

Would Bianca SWINNEY have committed an offence of child abduction (contrary to s. 1 of the Child Abduction Act 1984) in these circumstances?

A No, as the offence relates to a child under the age of 14 (and Rebecca is 15 years old).
B No, Bianca is named in a child arrangements order as a person with whom Rebecca will live and she has taken her out of the United Kingdom for a period of less than one month.
C Yes, the offence is complete when Bianca takes Rebecca to Scotland.
D Yes, the offence is complete when Bianca takes Rebecca to Norway.

42. Paul and Kelly MIDWOOD (both 39 years old) are married and live in a house together with Kelly MIDWOOD's 60-year-old mother LOGDON. The relationship between Paul and Kelly MIDWOOD has deteriorated, resulting in Paul MIDWOOD threatening violence towards Kelly MIDWOOD on several occasions. LOGDON has witnessed the threats being made and contacts the police who attend the house during an argument between Paul and Kelly MIDWOOD; the police witness Paul MIDWOOD threatening violence towards Kelly MIDWOOD. As a result, the police consider that issuing a Domestic Violence Protection Notice (DVPN) under s. 24 of the Crime and Security Act 2010 is necessary to protect Kelly MIDWOOD.

In relation to the issuing of such a DVPN, which of the following comments is correct?

A If Kelly MIDWOOD does not consent to the issuing of a DVPN, then a DVPN cannot be issued.
B The officer authorising the DVPN must consider any representations made by Paul MIDWOOD as to the issuing of a DVPN.
C If a DVPN is issued, then the authorising officer must apply to a magistrates' court for a Domestic Violence Protection Order (DVPO) no later than 24 hours after the DVPN was issued.
D A DVPN could not require Paul MIDWOOD to leave the house he lives in with Kelly MIDWOOD.

43. MURRAY (a resident of the United Kingdom) goes on a business trip to Turkey. During his trip, he is in a restaurant when he overhears a conversation between two men who are talking about planting a bomb at Heathrow Airport in a month's time. The men state that the bomb will kill hundreds of people and that when it explodes they will claim it as a victory for al-Qaeda against the British government. MURRAY believes that the information he has heard could help to prevent an act of terrorism. MURRAY flies home to England two days later but does not say anything to anyone about the conversation he overheard in Turkey.

With regard to the offence of information about acts of terrorism (contrary to s. 38B of the Terrorism Act 2000), which of the following comments is correct?

A MURRAY must disclose the information as soon as reasonably practicable and this disclosure can be made to any person in authority.
B As MURRAY was outside the country when he became aware of the information, he could not be charged with this offence if he failed to disclose that information.
C MURRAY would commit this offence as he believes the information he has might be of material assistance in preventing an act of terrorism.
D MURRAY has committed this offence to which there is no defence.

44. CRAMPTON is waiting to be served at a fish and chip shop owned by PAPACOSTAS (a Cypriot national). The pair chat and during their conversation PAPACOSTAS tells CRAMPTON that he is Cypriot. CRAMPTON leaves the shop with his food and walks home. When he gets home, he finds out that he has been given the wrong order and rather than cod and chips he has been given two small fishcakes. CRAMPTON is livid and goes back to the fish and chip shop which is now closed. In a fit of temper because he has been given the wrong food, CRAMPTON smashes the front window of the fish and chip shop. He leaves the scene and walks back to his home but is stopped by the police 20 minutes later and is arrested on suspicion of committing criminal damage. On arrest, he says, *'Those Cypriot bastards are always stealing our money, I can say what I like about them—it's a free country.'*

Considering the law relating to s. 28 of the Crime and Disorder Act 1998 (racially or religiously aggravated offences) and in particular a 'demonstration' of hostility, which of the following comments is correct?

A Demonstrating racial hostility 20 minutes after the criminal damage would not amount to an aggravated offence (it is not 'immediately after' a trigger offence).
B A demonstration of hostility must be immediately before or at the time of committing a trigger offence—a demonstration of hostility after the commission of a trigger offence would not be covered by the legislation.
C A demonstration of hostility must take place in the presence of the victim to be racially and/or religiously aggravated.
D A demonstration of hostility associated with an offence of criminal damage must take place at the time of the criminal damage.

45. LAMBERT is holding a party at his house and has drunk a bottle of gin and is drunk. He decides to set out an obstacle course in his large, private rear garden and challenges his party guests to drive a motorbike (a mechanically propelled vehicle) as fast as they can through the obstacles. Several party guests drive through the course before LAMBERT takes his turn. LAMBERT is determined to win and accelerates the motorbike to a speed of 50 mph, but as he is going through one of the obstacles a 5-year-old child of one of the party guests runs out in front of him. As LAMBERT is drunk, his reactions are slow and he cannot avoid the child and hits the child causing serious head injuries to the child in the process. The child is rushed to hospital but later dies as a result of the serious head injuries.

Could LAMBERT be convicted of an offence of causing death by dangerous driving (contrary to s. 1 of the Road Traffic Act 1988) in these circumstances?

A Yes, and the fact that LAMBERT was adversely affected by alcohol is, in itself, determinative to prove the offence.
B No, because the death occurred when the child was at a hospital rather than while LAMBERT was driving the motorbike.
C Yes, and evidence of drink will be admissible where the quantity of it may have adversely affected the quality of LAMBERT's driving.
D No, as the accident took place on private land rather than a road or public place.

46. Police officers visit the home address of RHODES and arrest him on suspicion of committing an offence of child abduction (contrary to s. 2 of the Child Abduction Act 1984). Whilst RHODES remains on the premises, the officers search his home address and in the process recover a rifle which fires 7.62 mm bullets and an imitation revolver.

In respect of the offence of possessing a firearm while committing or being arrested for a sch. 1 offence (contrary to s. 17(2) of the Firearms Act 1968), which of the following statements is correct?

A RHODES commits the offence but this would only be in connection with the rifle.
B The offence is not committed as child abduction is not a sch. 1 offence.
C The offence is committed in respect of the rifle and the imitation firearm.
D RHODES can only be found guilty of the s. 17(2) Firearms Act offence if he is found guilty of the child abduction offence first.

47. DEVINE and SURTEES are extremists who are opposed to the activities of a large fast-food chain. The two decide to attack one of the fast-food restaurants and cause damage to the premises. DEVINE buys a number of large fireworks which he intends to fire at the restaurants and cause damage; he stores these in the kitchen of his flat. SURTEES buys several petrol bombs which she intends to throw at the premises and cause damage; she stores these in a lock-up garage that she rents which is 10 miles from her home.

Would these activities amount to an offence under s. 4 of the Explosives Act 1883 (making or possessing explosives under suspicious circumstances)?

A No, fireworks and petrol bombs are not 'explosive substances' for the purposes of the Explosives Act 1883.
B Yes, but only DEVINE would commit the offence in these circumstances.
C No, as the items are going to be used to damage property rather than cause injury to people.
D Yes, DEVINE and SURTEES would commit the offence in these circumstances.

48. KENDALL works for a sales company and is considering setting up his own rival business. In order to give his fledgling business a good start, KENDALL gains unauthorised access to his manager's computer (committing an offence under s. 1 of the Computer Misuse Act 1990 in the process, i.e. 'hacking') intending to write down business-related information contained on his manager's computer screen detailing a large number of influential business contacts.

Is this an offence of unauthorised access with intent to commit further offences (contrary to s. 2 of the Computer Misuse Act 1990)?

A No, because this offence under s. 2 relates to obtaining information for another person to use in the commission of an offence.
B Yes, as KENDALL has committed an offence of 'unauthorised access' (under s. 1 of the Act) with the relevant intent.
C No, as KENDALL's activities do not constitute an offence to which this section applies.
D Yes, but KENDALL must actually obtain and make use of the information before the offence is complete.

49. TIMPSON commits an offence of theft from a supermarket. The police are called and PC YALE attends the scene and arrests TIMPSON. TIMPSON struggles against the arrest and GANGAR (a customer in the supermarket) sees this and does nothing to help the officer. PC YALE shouts out for help and GANGAR decides to assist the officer to deal with TIMPSON, and he runs over and joins the struggle. As all three are pulling and pushing in opposite directions, it actually turns out that GANGAR is, accidentally, of no help to PC YALE and GANGAR's intervention actually enables TIMPSON to escape from the supermarket.

Does GANGAR commit the offence of obstructing a police officer (contrary to s. 89(2) of the Police Act 1996)?

A No, GANGAR must either intend to obstruct a police officer in the lawful execution of his/her duty or be reckless as to whether the officer will be obstructed.
B Yes, when GANGAR saw the officer struggling and did nothing to help.
C Yes, when GANGAR accidentally made it harder for the officer to carry out the lawful execution of his duty.
D No, GANGAR did not wilfully obstruct PC YALE.

50. The police receive a large amount of good quality intelligence from a number of reliable sources that over the course of the next three days there will be a huge amount of drug dealing taking place at an open-air music festival. The police deploy a number of resources to deal with the situation, including several undercover officers; DC POPAT is one of those undercover police officers. At the festival, DC POPAT is approached by BARBER who says to the officer, *'Can you sell me some cannabis mate?'* DC POPAT replies *'No, I'm not a drug dealer, pal.'* BARBER then says, *'It's your lucky day because I am—do you want to buy some cannabis?'* BARBER never actually intended to buy or sell any drugs and does not in fact have any cannabis to sell; he has approached DC POPAT as he is suspicious of him and has identified him as an undercover police officer.

At what stage, if at all, does BARBER first commit an offence under the Misuse of Drugs Act 1971?

A When he asks DC POPAT to sell him some cannabis.
B When he offers to supply cannabis to the officer.
C At no point as the comments are made to an undercover police officer.
D At no point because he never intended to buy or sell any drugs.

51. ROSE is an electrician and visits a Catholic church to carry out some minor repairs on a faulty switch. As ROSE walks out of the church, BOTTING sees him and presumes ROSE to be a Catholic. BOTTING intensely dislikes Catholics and decides to damage ROSE's property because of his hostility towards them. He follows ROSE to his van and, as ROSE is opening the van door, BOTTING kicks the van door causing criminal damage to it (contrary to s. 1(1) of the Criminal Damage Act 1971). In fact, ROSE is a Protestant.

Based on these circumstances alone, has BOTTING committed a religiously aggravated offence?

A Yes, the offence is motivated by religious hostility.
B No, as ROSE is not a Catholic.
C Yes, all offences under the Criminal Damage Act 1971 can be racially and/or religiously aggravated.
D No, there has been no demonstration of hostility from BOTTING.

52. GARCIA is fascinated by Adolf Hitler and the Nazi Party and their treatment and extermination of millions of people in concentration camps in the 1930s and 1940s. He has a collection of Nazi memorabilia on display in the rear living room of his house, including a large swastika flag which has 'Tod der Juden!' ('Death to Jews!') written on it. AKERMAN (who is a Jew) sees the flag and words written on it when he is standing in the rear bedroom of a house that backs on to GARCIA's house. AKERMAN is extremely upset at what he sees and contacts the police.

Has GARCIA committed an offence under s. 29B of the Public Order Act 1986 (use of words or behaviour or display of written material)?

A Yes, although GARCIA would have a defence if he believed the flag on display could not be seen by a person outside his dwelling.
B No, as the written material is displayed by a person inside a dwelling and not seen except by other persons in that or another dwelling.
C Yes, as the flag is threatening and can be seen from outside GARCIA's dwelling.
D No, not unless GARCIA intends to stir up religious hatred.

53. WHITE and THURSTON are long-term partners and have been living together in the same house for 20 years. WHITE finds out that THURSTON has been having an affair with a work colleague and is fuming about the situation, although she has not confronted THURSTON about the affair as she is unsure how to handle the situation. A week after finding out about the affair, THURSTON is having a bath at the shared house and WHITE is in the living room downstairs drinking whisky. WHITE has drunk nearly the whole bottle of whisky and is very drunk. She becomes exceptionally angry about THURSTON's affair and decides to confront him about it. She goes into the kitchen, grabs a kitchen knife and takes it upstairs and goes into the bathroom. Holding the kitchen knife, WHITE issues a drunken threat to kill THURSTON (there is no one else in the house at this time).

Considering only the offence of affray (contrary to s. 3 of the Public Order Act 1986) and the case law relating to it, which of the following comments is correct?

A The offence of affray is not committed as the activity is taking place in private.
B The offence of affray is not committed as there is only one person (rather than the required two or more persons) threatening unlawful violence.
C The offence of affray has not been committed as WHITE threatened rather than used violence.
D The offence of affray has not been committed because there is no possibility of a hypothetical bystander fearing for their safety.

54. ANDERTON (aged 13 years) has been convicted of an offence of supplying a controlled drug (contrary to s. 4(3) of the Misuse of Drugs Act 1971). The officer in the case is DC COLEMAN who has evidence that suggests that the conviction came about because ANDERTON was involved with four other persons who identify themselves as the 'Blue Cap' gang (identifiable by the fact that they wear blue baseball caps) who are heavily involved with drug-related activities. A work colleague suggests to DC COLEMAN that the police could apply for an injunction under s. 34 of the Policing and Crime Act 2009 to prevent ANDERTON from engaging in gang related drug-dealing activity.

Could such an injunction be granted in these circumstances?

A No, as ANDERTON is only 13 years old.
B Yes, as long as the court to which the application is made is satisfied beyond all reasonable doubt that ANDERTON has engaged in gang-related drug-dealing activity.
C No, as this is not 'gang-related' (a 'gang' consists of five or more people).
D Yes, and if granted the court must attach a power of arrest to any prohibition or requirement in the injunction.

55. WALKER is walking through an exclusive men's clothes section of a large department store. As he is browsing, he hears NICKLIN and JAKEMAN (members of staff) chatting to each other. He hears NICKLIN say how frightened she is of dark enclosed spaces. WALKER waits until NICKLIN and JAKEMAN separate and approaches NICKLIN. WALKER says, *'Get that Prada shirt and meet me outside in 5 minutes because if you don't I'll wait for you after you finish work and lock you in the boot of my car.'* NICKLIN is petrified because of her fear of confined spaces. At that moment, JAKEMAN reappears and WALKER says to him, *'You can meet me outside as well and bring an expensive shirt. If you don't, I'll kick your head in this evening!'*

Considering only the offence of blackmail (under s. 21 of the Theft Act 1968), which of the following comments is correct?

A The offence has been committed, but only in relation to NICKLIN.
B The offence has been committed, but only in relation to JAKEMAN.
C The offence has been committed in relation to NICKLIN and JAKEMAN.
D The offence of blackmail has not been committed in these circumstances.

56. BAYODE's wife has been having an affair with O'LEARY—BAYODE has found out and is fuming and wants to get revenge on O'LEARY. BAYODE owns a garage that has a large stock of car accessories including brake fluid which BAYODE knows will destroy the paint on O'LEARY's car and he intends to use the brake fluid to do so—he plans to do this early tomorrow morning. BAYODE is at his house on his mobile phone boasting to a friend about what he intends to do when his wife overhears the conversation and informs the police of BAYODE's intention.

In relation to the offence under s. 3 of the Criminal Damage Act 1971 (having articles with intent to destroy or damage property) and the power under s. 6 of the Act in relation to warrants to search for such items, which of the following comments is correct?

A The offence is committed and the police can apply for a warrant to search BAYODE's garage for the brake fluid he intends to use to cause criminal damage.
B The offence is not committed as BAYODE does not have the brake fluid 'with him'.
C The offence is not committed because BAYODE does not possess the thing with the intention of endangering the life of another.
D The offence is committed, although a warrant could not be obtained to search for the brake fluid unless it had actually been used to cause criminal damage.

57. HILLIER knocks on the door of a house owned by PEACH. HILLIER tells PEACH that he was walking past PEACH's house and noticed that the roof was in need of emergency repairs. HILLIER tells PEACH that it will not cost much (only £150) and he is in a position to do the work immediately but only if PEACH pays him £150 there and then. PEACH gives HILLIER £150 and HILLIER promises PEACH that he will start the work immediately and states that he will go and get his tools and the equipment to carry out the repairs as he has these in his van which he has parked nearby. HILLIER walks off and does not return; the truth of the matter is that HILLIER never intended to carry out the work.

In relation to the offence of fraud by false representation (contrary to s. 2 of the Fraud Act 2006), which of the following comments is correct?

A The offence has not been committed as the representation that is false must be one as to fact or law—this is a broken promise.
B The offence has been committed as HILLIER's statement (that he will repair the roof) is false—it misrepresents his actual intentions as he never intended to keep the promise he made.
C The offence has been committed although it will be tried summarily as this is low-value fraud (the value of the goods fraudulently obtained does not exceed £200).
D The offence has been committed but would only be complete when PEACH gave HILLIER the £150.

58. XAVIER is a homeless person who travels from place to place, sleeping in the streets. On a particularly cold night, XAVIER becomes concerned that he may die from hypothermia so, purely to obtain shelter from the cold, he breaks into a warehouse office. Once inside the office, he turns on an electric fire to warm himself up. Having warmed up, he decides to look around the office to see if there is anything worth stealing and, after a short search, he finds a jar containing approximately £30 in change which he steals. Curious about the premises he is in, he moves from the warehouse office through a door into a room marked 'Stores'. He walks around the store for several minutes before becoming bored and frustrated at his lot in life and he damages a sink unit in the store. As he is about to leave, he sees a small box containing a number of batteries and, thinking he will be able to sell them, he steals them.

At what stage does XAVIER first commit an offence of burglary under s. 9(1)(a) or s. 9(1)(b) of the Theft Act 1968?

A A burglary offence is first committed when XAVIER turns on the electric fire.
B A burglary offence is first committed when XAVIER steals the £30 in change.
C A burglary offence is first committed when XAVIER damages the sink.
D A burglary offence is first committed when XAVIER steals the batteries.

59. EISEMAN has been arrested for large-scale fraud relating to the use of credit cards over an extended period of time and enabling him to obtain goods worth approximately £3 million. He is taken to a designated police station and a s. 18 PACE authorisation is given to search his house. When officers search the house, they recover a number of items including a computer that EISEMAN has used to carry out the fraud offences. Analysis of the computer leads to the discovery of a computer program that EISEMAN used to generate credit card numbers to carry out the fraud offences and also a computer template that EISEMAN used for producing blank utility bills when committing the fraud offences.

Does EISEMAN commit an offence of possession or control of articles for use in frauds (contrary to s. 6 of the Fraud Act 2006)?

A Yes, but only in relation to the computer program that generates credit card numbers.
B No, as these items were recovered on a computer that was in EISEMAN's home.
C Yes, in relation to the computer program that generates credit card numbers and the template that can be used for producing blank utility bills.
D No, as these articles are related to fraud offences that have already taken place.

60. SHACKLOCK has been charged with an offence of handling stolen goods (contrary to s. 22 of the Theft Act 1968). SHACKLOCK has a previous conviction for theft which precedes the date of the handling offence by four years. The police also have evidence that SHACKLOCK had stolen property in his possession from a theft that preceded the handling offence by nine months (he was never charged with an offence relating to that incident).

Which of the following comments is correct in respect of the ability of the prosecution to utilise s. 27 of the Theft Act 1968 (admissibility of previous misconduct for the purpose of proving SHACKLOCK knew or believed the goods to be stolen goods)?

A Provided that seven days' notice in writing is given to SHACKLOCK, the previous conviction is admissible as is the evidence that he was in possession of stolen property nine months ago.
B Provided that seven days' notice in writing is given to SHACKLOCK, the previous conviction is admissible; the evidence that he was in possession of stolen property nine months ago is inadmissible.
C The previous conviction is inadmissible; the evidence that he was in possession of stolen property nine months ago is admissible.
D The previous conviction and the evidence that he was in possession of stolen property nine months ago are both inadmissible.

61. DUNN and WRIGHT enter a bank. DUNN approaches a cashier and hands over a note which states, '*Look right—near to the window*'. The cashier looks to his right and, on the other side of the bank, the cashier can see WRIGHT (DUNN's accomplice) holding a gun pointing towards the back of an old-age pensioner who is a customer at the bank. The old-age pensioner is completely unaware of the fact that WRIGHT has a gun towards his back. DUNN passes another note to the cashier which states, '*Hand over all the money or he gets shot!*' The cashier refuses. DUNN speaks to WRIGHT and says '*Do it!*' WRIGHT strikes the back of the old-age pensioner's head with the butt of the gun. The customer falls to the ground and WRIGHT points the gun at the customer. DUNN looks at the cashier and states, '*Do you think I'm joking? Hand over the money or he gets shot!*' The cashier, fearing for the customer, hands over a large amount of cash.

At what point, if at all, has the offence of robbery been committed?

A When DUNN passes over the first note and the cashier can see the gun being pointed towards the back of the customer.
B When DUNN passes over the second note demanding the money.
C When the cashier hands over a large amount of cash.
D The offence of robbery has not been committed in these circumstances.

62. DOWNING is the tenant of a house rented from BAKER. The rented house has a rear garden which is separated by a small wooden fence from the garden of a house owned by STEBBING. On the last day of DOWNING's tenancy agreement, she is standing in the back garden of her rented house and looking at some raspberries growing wild in STEBBING's rear garden. She decides she will pick and eat some of the raspberries and climbs over the fence into STEBBING's garden and picks a dozen raspberries. She climbs back into her rented garden and looks at a dwarf Korean lilac tree that BAKER has planted—DOWNING has always admired the tree so decides to dig it up and take it with her to her new house.

What is DOWNING's liability in relation to the offence of theft (contrary to s. 1(1) of the Theft Act 1968)?

A DOWNING is liable for theft but only in relation to the raspberries picked from STEBBING's garden.
B DOWNING is liable for theft but only in relation to the dwarf Korean lilac tree.
C DOWNING is liable for theft in relation to the raspberries picked from STEBBING's garden and the dwarf Korean lilac tree.
D DOWNING would not commit an offence of theft in these circumstances.

72. COOPER approaches GAYLE who is standing alone at a bus stop in the early hours of the morning. COOPER tells GAYLE to stand still, be quiet and let him touch her or he will stab her. GAYLE is extremely frightened and does not do anything as COOPER takes a rolled up newspaper and uses it to touch her breasts through her clothes.

Would this amount to an offence of sexual touching (contrary to s. 3 of the Sexual Offences Act 2003)?

A Yes, and the evidential presumptions under s. 75 of the Sexual Offences Act 2003 would be relevant in the circumstances.
B No, COOPER did not touch GAYLE or anyone else with a part of his body.
C Yes, although the evidential presumptions under s. 75 of the Sexual Offences Act 2003 would not be relevant in the circumstances
D No, because COOPER touched GAYLE through her clothes.

73. COULTON (aged 17) has accompanied his mother to a care home to visit SPENCER (a 57-year-old family friend who suffers from cerebral palsy). COULTON's mother leaves the room SPENCER lives in to make a phone call, leaving COULTON in the room with SPENCER. COULTON decides that he will sexually assault SPENCER and intentionally touches her breasts through her clothing—SPENCER is unable to refuse the sexual touching because of her mental condition and COULTON is thoroughly aware of this.

Does COULTON commit an offence of sexual activity with a person with a mental disorder (contrary to s. 30 of the Sexual Offences Act 2003)?

A No, as COULTON is under 18 years of age.
B Yes, as long as COULTON touches SPENCER to obtain sexual gratification.
C No, as the activity does not involve penetration.
D Yes, all the elements of the offence are present.

74. KNIGHT (a 47-year-old male) establishes contact with BELL (a 15-year-old female) using an internet video communication service. KNIGHT lies about his age to BELL telling her that he is 15 years old, but he manages to get away with this by telling BELL his webcam has a fault and covering it so that he cannot be seen (although he can be heard). During the conversation, KNIGHT tells BELL how old he is and removes the cover on the webcam so that BELL can see him. He then asks BELL if she is 'still a virgin' and then begins to masturbate in front of the camera. KNIGHT does this to obtain sexual gratification and also intending BELL to obtain sexual gratification from watching him masturbate.

Which of the following comments is correct in relation to the offence of engaging in sexual activity in the presence of a child (contrary to s. 11 of the Sexual Offences Act 2003)?

A The offence is committed because KNIGHT intends BELL to obtain sexual gratification from seeing him masturbate.
B The activity must take place in the physical presence of the child; this has not occurred, so the offence is incomplete.
C KNIGHT commits the offence in these circumstances.
D The offence is not committed as BELL is 15 years old (it must be in the hearing and/or presence of a child under 13).

75. FOGG is an 18-year-old male and his new girlfriend is WAITE, a 15-year-old female (FOGG is aware of WAITE's age). They have been going out together for a couple of weeks. WAITE is very shy and knows very little about sex. FOGG decides that the only way he is going to be able to have sex with WAITE is to show her pictures of a pornographic nature to lower her inhibitions so that he can achieve sexual gratification at a later date. FOGG at first shows WAITE cartoon still images of persons having sexual intercourse. Then a day later he shows her moving cartoons of persons having sexual intercourse. A week later, as WAITE is now showing more interest, FOGG shows her a pornographic video involving sexual intercourse between males and females via the internet. FOGG believes that after this showing she will have sex with him. WAITE is not amused by this and tells him their relationship is over.

Considering the offence under s. 12 of the Sexual Offences Act 2003 (causing a child to watch a sex act), when if at all does FOGG first commit the offence?

A FOGG does not commit the offence as no sexual gratification was obtained whilst WAITE was exposed to the pornography.
B FOGG commits the offence when he showed her the internet pornography as that was when he believed he would obtain sexual gratification.
C FOGG commits the offence when he shows the moving cartoon pornography.
D FOGG commits the offence when he shows WAITE the first pornographic cartoon still image.

76. NIJAL was attacked by BANKS who attempted to subject NIJAL to a sexual assault which would have amounted to an offence under s. 2 of the Sexual Offences Act 2003 (assault by penetration). NIJAL fought BANKS off and BANKS was later arrested and charged with an attempt to commit assault by penetration (under the Criminal Attempts Act 1981). NIJAL is extremely concerned about her identity becoming known and the stigma she feels this will bring to her in the local community. She approaches the officer in the case, DC LITTLEWOOD, for some advice regarding anonymity.

In relation to anonymity and the provisions of s. 1 of the Sexual Offences (Amendment) Act 1992, which of the following statements is correct?

A NIJAL would not be entitled to anonymity under the Act as this only applies to victims of an offence of rape (contrary to s. 1 of the Sexual Offences Act 2003).
B NIJAL would be entitled to anonymity throughout her lifetime and this would be the case even if proceedings against BANKS were later abandoned.
C NIJAL would be entitled to anonymity for a period of 20 years beginning with the date that BANKS is accused of the offence.
D NIJAL would not be entitled to anonymity under the Act as BANKS has not been charged with an offence under the Sexual Offences Act 2003—he has been charged with an attempt to commit such an act.

77. POMFRET is at a house party and has been drinking so heavily that she has fallen unconscious. Her friends take her to a bedroom in the house and leave her in a bed to sleep for the rest of the night. FARRELL and ALLEN have seen what has happened and go into the bedroom where POMFRET is sleeping and remove POMFRET's clothing. FARRELL takes hold of POMFRET's hand and places one of her fingers in his anus while ALLEN puts his penis in POMFRET's mouth.

Considering only the offence of assault by penetration (contrary to s. 2 of the Sexual Offences Act 2003), which of the comments below is correct?

A The offence has not been committed in these circumstances.
B FARRELL has committed the offence, ALLEN has not.
C ALLEN has committed the offence, FARRELL has not.
D FARRELL and ALLEN have committed the offence.

78. BROWN and MAUNSELL have been going out together for several weeks. BROWN has suggested sexual intercourse to MAUNSELL but she has politely refused him; this has annoyed BROWN. The pair pay a visit to a restaurant for a meal and during the meal BROWN sees a member of staff (CURRIN) serving drinks at the restaurant bar. BROWN knows CURRIN very well and approaches him and offers him £200 to put large amounts of alcohol in the cocktails that MAUNSELL is drinking (MAUNSELL does not drink alcohol and is drinking non-alcoholic cocktails). BROWN's intention is to get MAUNSELL drunk so that he can have sexual intercourse with her. CURRIN asks BROWN why he wants him to put alcohol in MAUNSELL's drink and, when BROWN tells him, he thinks it is funny and agrees to do as BROWN requests. Over a period of three hours, MAUNSELL becomes very drunk and is violently sick, so much so that the staff at the restaurant call for an ambulance and she is taken to hospital; meaning that BROWN does not have the opportunity to have sexual intercourse with her.

In relation to the offence of administering a substance with intent (contrary to s. 61 of the Sexual Offences Act 2003), which of the following statements is correct?

A 'Spiking' MAUNSELL's soft drink with alcohol would not amount to an offence under s. 2 of the Act (alcohol is not a 'substance').
B CURRIN does not commit the offence as the alcohol was introduced to MAUNSELL's non-alcoholic drink so that BROWN (rather than CURRIN) could engage in sexual activity with MAUNSELL.
C BROWN and CURRIN would commit the offence in this situation.
D Only CURRIN would commit the offence in this situation.

79. DCs ZAFAR and WILLIAMSON are attending a training course primarily directed towards the investigation of sexual offences and the associated law under the Sexual Offences Act 2003. During the course, legislation and case law relating to the offence of rape is being discussed and the officers make a number of comments regarding the offence.

Which one of the comments made by the officers shows a correct understanding of the law?

A DC ZAFAR states that an offence of rape would be committed if a male falsely represented to a female that he had had a vasectomy and she agrees to unprotected sexual intercourse as a result of the representation.
B DC WILLIAMSON states that if a man deceived a woman into having sexual intercourse more frequently than she would have done otherwise, this would amount to an offence of rape.
C DC ZAFAR states that if a male told a female prostitute that he would pay her for sexual intercourse but it is a false promise to pay and he does not pay her, this would amount to an offence of rape.
D DC WILLIAMSON states that an offence of rape would be committed if a male falsely assures a female that he is wearing a condom when he is not and she agrees to unprotected sexual intercourse as a result of the representation.

80. TOLHURST is lawfully stopped and searched by PC MOSES under s. 1 of the Police and Criminal Evidence Act 1984. During the course of the search, PC MOSES finds several photographs in TOLHURST's possession which show a naked 18-year-old male exposing his genitals in a variety of poses. TOLHURST tells the officer he was given the pictures by the person in the photograph and keeps them for his own sexual gratification.

Would possession of the photographs amount to an offence under s. 1 of the Protection of Children Act 1978 or s. 160 of the Criminal Justice Act 1988 (offences relating to indecent photographs of children)?

A No, as the image is not 'pornographic'.
B No, as the person in the pictures is 18 years old.
C No, as TOLHURST did not take/make the photographs.
D No, as TOLHURST is not going to distribute the photographs.

OXFORD
UNIVERSITY PRESS

Blackstone's Police Investigators' Mock Examination Paper 2025

Pack 2

Contents

DO NOT OPEN THIS ANSWER PACK UNTIL YOU HAVE COMPLETED THE MOCK EXAM

OXFORD UNIVERSITY PRESS	Blackstone's Police Investigators' Mock Examination Paper 2025

Marking Instructions

Lay your answer sheet next to the marking matrix and begin the marking process.

Starting with Question 1, compare your marked answer with the correct answer given in the marking matrix. If the correct answer matches your marked answer put a '✓' mark inside the white box on the relevant row (see questions 1, 2 and 4 below). If it does not (see Question 3) put an '✗' mark.

Question	Answer	General Principles, Police Powers and Procedures	Random Non-counting MCQ
1	D	✓	
2	C	✓	
3	A	✗	
4	C		✓

The first 35 questions in the Mock Examination all relate to Part 1 of the syllabus, 'General Principles, Police Powers and Procedures'; however, you will see that not all of the 35 questions will count towards your mark as 6 questions within this block of 35 have been designated as a 'Random Non-counting MCQ'. This is in order to reflect the nature of the marking process used in your NIE.

When you have marked the first 35 questions, add up the total for the 'General Principles, Police Powers and Procedures' column to give you a mark out of 29.

34	A	✓	
35	D	✗	
Total	=	18/29	

Then do the same for Questions 36 to 54 ('Serious Crime and Other Offences'), Questions 55 to 66 ('Property Offences') and Questions 67 to 80 ('Sexual Offences').

Enter the totals for each block of questions in the 'Final Score' table and add them up to reach a final total (out of 70) for the whole exam.

Compare your final score to the table underneath the 'Final Score', which will indicate whether or not you have passed the mock examination. The pass mark for the exam is 39.

Marking Matrix, Questions 1–35

Question	Answer	General Principles, Police Powers and Procedures	Random Non-counting MCQ
1	D		
2	C		
3	A		
4	C		
5	C		
6	D		
7	B		
8	A		
9	B		
10	A		
11	C		
12	B		
13	B		
14	A		
15	C		
16	D		
17	C		
18	D		
19	B		
20	A		
21	A		
22	A		
23	C		
24	B		
25	A		
26	C		
27	B		
28	B		
29	C		
30	D		
31	A		
32	D		
33	B		
34	A		
35	A		
Total	=	/29	

Marking Matrix, Questions 36–54

Question	Answer	Serious Crime and Other Offences	Random Non-counting MCQ
36	B		
37	D		
38	C		
39	A		
40	A		
41	B		
42	B		
43	C		
44	A		
45	D		
46	C		
47	D		
48	C		
49	D		
50	A		
51	A		
52	B		
53	D		
54	A		
Total	=	/18	

Marking Matrix, Questions 55–66

Question	Answer	Property Offences	Random Non-counting MCQ
55	C		
56	A		
57	B		
58	B		
59	D		
60	A		
61	C		
62	D		
63	C		
64	A		
65	A		
66	D		
Total	=	/10	

Marking Matrix, Questions 67–80

Question	Answer	Sexual Offences	Random Non-counting MCQ
67	B		
68	A		
69	A		
70	B		
71	D		
72	A		
73	D		
74	C		
75	D		
76	B		
77	A		
78	C		
79	D		
80	B		
Total	=	/13	

Final Score

Syllabus Area	*Marks*
General Principles etc.	**/29**
Serious Crime and Other Offences	**/18**
Property Offences	**/10**
Sexual Offences	**/13**
TOTAL =	**/70**

Questions right	% score	Questions right	% score	Questions right	% score	Questions right	% score	Questions right	% score
1	1.429	15	21.429	29	41.429	43	61.429	57	81.429
2	2.857	16	22.857	30	42.857	44	62.857	58	82.857
3	4.286	17	24.286	31	44.286	45	64.286	59	84.286
4	5.714	18	25.714	32	45.714	46	65.714	60	85.714
5	7.143	19	27.143	33	47.143	47	67.143	61	87.143
6	8.571	20	28.571	34	48.571	48	68.571	62	88.571
7	10	21	30	35	50	49	70	63	90
8	11.429	22	31.429	36	51.429	50	71.429	64	91.429
9	12.857	23	32.857	37	52.857	51	72.857	65	92.857
10	14.286	24	34.286	38	54.286	52	74.286	66	94.286
11	15.714	25	35.714	39	55.714	53	75.714	67	95.714
12	17.143	26	37.143	40	57.143	54	77.143	68	97.143
13	18.571	27	38.571	41	58.571	55	78.571	69	98.571
14	20	28	40	42	60	56	80	70	100

OXFORD UNIVERSITY PRESS	**Blackstone's Police Investigators' Mock Examination Paper 2025**

Answer Booklet

1. Answer **D** — Code E of the Codes of Practice, para. 1.13 states:

   Nothing in this Code requires the identity of officers or police staff conducting interviews to be recorded or disclosed if the interviewer reasonably believes recording or disclosing their name might put them in danger. In these cases, the officers and staff should use warrant or other identification numbers and the name of their police station. Such instances and the reasons for them shall be recorded in the custody record or the interviewer's pocket book.

   This is relevant to visually recorded interviews where, at para. 2.7 of Code F we are told that:

   In cases to which paragraph 1.13 of Code E (disclosure of identity of officers or police staff conducting interviews) applies:

   (a) the officers and staff may have their backs to the visual recording device; and
   (b) when in accordance with Code E paragraph 3.21 or 4.12 as they apply to this Code, arrangements are made for the suspect to have access to the visual recording, the investigating officer may arrange for anything in the recording that might allow the officers or police staff to be identified to be concealed.

   Therefore answer D is correct and answers A, B and C are incorrect.

   Investigators' Manual, paras 1.9.7, 1.9.13

2. Answer **C** — An arrest warrant can be issued for a suspect by a justice of the peace if an information in writing is laid before them that a person has committed or is suspected of having committed an offence (s. 1(1)(b) and (3) of the Magistrates' Courts Act 1980). Such warrants can only be issued for persons aged 18 or over (answer A is incorrect) if the offence the warrant relates to is an indictable offence or is punishable with imprisonment or the person's address is not sufficiently established for a summons or written charge and requisition to be served on him/her (s. 1(4)) (answer B is incorrect—the offence under s. 2A of the Protection from Harassment Act 1997 is punishable by imprisonment (six months)). Section 125 of the Act deals with the execution of warrants and provides that a warrant of arrest issued by a justice of the peace shall remain in force until it is executed or withdrawn or it ceases to have effect in accordance with rules of court (s. 125(1)) so answer D is incorrect and answer C is correct.

   Investigators' Manual, para. 1.4.5

their arrest and not the time of arrival at the police station, making answer C incorrect. The period may not be interrupted or delayed, except:

(a) when there are reasonable grounds for believing not delaying or interrupting the period would:
  (i) involve a risk of harm to people or serious loss of, or damage to, property;
  (ii) delay unnecessarily the person's release from custody; or
  (iii) otherwise prejudice the outcome of the investigation;
(b) at the request of the detainee, their appropriate adult or legal representative;
(c) when a delay or interruption is necessary in order to:
  (i) comply with the legal obligations and duties arising under section 15; or
  (ii) to take action required under *section 9* or in accordance with medical advice.

So answer D is incorrect as while para. 12.2(a)(i) is *one* of the reasons the rest period can be interrupted, it is one of many. Answer A is incorrect as para. 12.2(b) states that the rest period can be legitimately interrupted at the request of a legal representative. If the period is interrupted in accordance with sub-para. (a), a fresh period must be allowed. Interruptions under sub-paras (b) and (c) do not require a fresh period to be allowed (correct answer B).

Investigators' Manual, para. 1.9.4

10. Answer **A** — Whether or not a defendant is legally represented in an interview will not prevent adverse inferences being drawn (unless the defendant is being held incommunicado and legal advice has been withheld after the defendant has requested a solicitor), making answer D incorrect. A defendant cannot be convicted solely on an adverse inference drawn from silence, making answer B incorrect. Adverse inferences can be drawn from an interview where the suspect remains silent, responds 'no comment' to questioning or fails to mention any fact relied on in their defence in proceedings, making answer C incorrect.

Investigators' Manual, para. 1.9.2

11. Answer **C** — This is an excellent example of how the Blackstone's text provides core material for an MCQ. The text addresses the scenario where one party to a crime goes beyond that which was agreed or contemplated by the other. It provides an example where two men (A and B) agree to carry out an offence of theft. During the course of the offence, the owner of the property subject of the offence appears and tries to prevent the offence taking place. Offender A produces a flick-knife and stabs the victim, causing grievous bodily harm. Offender B had no idea that offender A had a flick-knife and had never contemplated the use of violence during the theft offence. The actions of offender A are a departure from the nature and type of crime that was envisaged by offender B who did not know that A possessed a flick-knife; it is an act so fundamentally different from that originally contemplated by B that B is most unlikely to be liable for the injuries caused to the victim (*R* v *Anderson* [1966] 2 QB 110). This would rule out KINCADE from liability in the MCQ and make answer D incorrect. The example goes on to state that the situation would alter if offender B knew that offender A possessed the flick-knife and encouraged A to use the flick-knife. Here, offender B could be convicted of a wounding offence if it can be proved that he had *intended* to assist or encourage the wounding offence. *Foresight* that the wounding might occur is simply evidence (albeit sometimes strong evidence) of intent to assist or encourage. It is a question for the jury

in every case whether the intention to assist or encourage is shown—a person is not to be taken to have had an intention merely because of foreseeability (this makes answer A and B incorrect and answer C correct).

Investigators' Manual, para. 1.3.8.2

12. Answer **B** — If a juvenile's parent is estranged from the juvenile, he/she should not be asked to act as the appropriate adult if the juvenile expressly and specifically objects to their presence (see Keynote to Code C 1.7), making answers A, C and D incorrect.

Investigators' Manual, para. 1.7.6

13. Answer **B** — A constable may require a person to attend a police station for the purpose of taking his/her fingerprints under s. 61(5A) when they have been arrested for a recordable offence and released, and the fingerprints that were taken were of insufficient quality (answer D is incorrect). If a person fails to comply with the requirement, that person can be arrested without warrant (answer A is incorrect). The person must be given a period of at least seven days within which to attend the police station (answer C is incorrect). If there is an urgent need for HARDCASTLE's fingerprints to be obtained for the purposes of the investigation of the offence, an officer of the rank of inspector or above may authorise a period shorter than seven days for HARDCASTLE to attend the police station (Annex G, para. 3—correct answer B).

Investigators' Manual, para. 1.8.14

14. Answer **A** — Section 25 of the Criminal Justice and Public Order Act 1994 applies when a defendant is charged with murder, attempted murder, manslaughter and a host of offences under the Sexual Offences Act 2003 and has a conviction for one of those offences. This makes answer D incorrect. There are no time limitations relating to when the previous conviction was obtained, making answer B incorrect. A defendant charged with one of the above offences, and with a previous conviction for one of the above offences, will not be granted bail unless there are exceptional circumstances which justify it, making answer C incorrect.

Investigators' Manual, para. 1.10.5

15. Answer **C** — Answer A is incorrect as Professional Standards Departments (PSDs) have final responsibility for the value judgement on whether information relating to misconduct of police officers should be revealed to the prosecutor. Answer D is incorrect as not only might the credibility of witnesses undermine the prosecution case, but so too might complaints against officers involved in the case, together with any occasions where officers have not been believed in court in the past. In these cases, it will be necessary to decide whether this information should be disclosed to the defence and, if disclosed, in how much detail. Advice given to prosecutors can assist when considering complaints and misconduct of police officers. The advice states:

    It is, of course, necessary in the first instance for the police to bring such matters to the notice of the prosecutor, but it is submitted that the prosecutor should have a greater element of discretion than with the disclosure of previous convictions. With convictions against prosecution witnesses, disclosure normally follows, whereas in relation to disciplinary findings regard should be had to the nature of the finding and its likely relevance to the matters in issue. Findings which involve some element of dishonesty should invariably be disclosed, while matters such as disobedience to orders, neglect of duty and discreditable conduct will often have no relevance to the officer's veracity or the guilt or otherwise of a defendant. Certainly, there should be no duty on the prosecution to disclose details of unsubstantiated complaints even though this is a popular type of inquiry from some defence representatives. The imposition of such a duty would only encourage the making of false complaints in the hope that they might be used to discredit an officer in the future.

There is no absolute requirement to disclose findings in relation to disciplinary matters (answer B is incorrect). Answer C is correct as per the above passage of text.

Investigators' Manual, para. 1.11.6.5

16. Answer **D** — Section 54A of the Police and Criminal Evidence Act 1984 provides a power to search and/or examine detained persons without their consent. This must be in order to ascertain whether the person has any mark that would tend to identify him/her as a person involved in the commission of an offence or to assist to identify him/her. Mark includes features and injuries. The search/examination is authorised by an officer of at least the rank of inspector. Authorisation may be given orally or in writing but if given orally it must be confirmed in writing as soon as possible.

Investigators' Manual, paras 1.8.6 to 1.8.6.1

17. Answer **C** — There is no specific provision within the Police and Criminal Evidence Act 1984 or the Codes of Practice for the disclosure of any information by the police at the police station, *with the exception of the custody record* (so the custody record must be disclosed, making answers A and B incorrect). In respect of the provision of a copy of the 'first description' of a suspect, it should be noted that Code D (para. 3.1) states that a copy of the 'first description' shall, where practicable, be given to the suspect or his/her solicitor before any procedures under paras 3.5 to 3.10, 3.21 or 3.23 are carried out. In other words, the disclosure requirement is that a copy of the 'first description' shall, where practicable, be given to the suspect or his/her solicitor before a video identification, an identification parade, a group identification or confrontation takes place. Therefore, an officer disclosing information to a solicitor at the interview stage (which is taking place in advance of any identification procedures) need not provide the 'first description' of a suspect at that time.

    Further, there is nothing within the Criminal Justice and Public Order Act 1994 that states that information must be disclosed before an inference from silence can be made (making answer D incorrect).

Investigators' Manual, para. 1.9.4

18. Answer **D** — There are a number of reasons that an interview may be recorded in writing. Code E, para. 2.3 states that a written record of the matters described in para. 2.1(a) and (b) shall be made in accordance with Code C, s. 11 if an authorised recording device in working order is not available (that is the case in this scenario) and (c) the 'relevant officer' described in para. 2.4 considers, on reasonable grounds, that the proposed interview or (as the case may be) continuation of the interview or other action, should not be delayed until an

authorised recording device in working order and a suitable interview room or other location become available and decides that a written record shall be made. Paragraph 2.4(c)(i) states that in the case of a voluntary interview which takes place at a police station and the offence in question is an indictable offence, the 'relevant officer' means an officer of the rank of sergeant or above, in consultation with the investigating officer—therefore the answer is D and answers A, B and C are incorrect.

Investigators' Manual, para. 1.9.8

19. Answer **B** — Code D deals with the process of taking footwear impressions in connection with a criminal investigation. Impressions of a person's footwear may be taken in connection with the investigation of an offence only with their consent or if para. 4.17 applies. If the person is at a police station, consent must be in writing. Paragraph 4.17 states that s. 61A of PACE provides the power for a police officer to take footwear impressions without consent from any person over the age of 10 years who is detained at a police station:

    (a) in consequence of being arrested for a recordable offence, or if the detainee has been charged with a recordable offence, or informed they will be reported for such an offence; and
    (b) the detainee has not had an impression of their footwear taken in the course of the investigation of the offence unless the previously taken impression is not complete or is not of sufficient quality to allow satisfactory analysis, comparison or matching (whether in the case in question or generally).

    This makes answers A and C incorrect (as the consent of GILBERT or O'TOOLE is not required). It is not necessary that the footprints are taken to prove or disprove the detained person's involvement in the offence, making answer D incorrect. Paragraph 4.18 of Code D states that reasonable force may be used, if necessary, to take a footwear impression from a detainee without consent under the power in para. 4.17 (correct answer B). A record must be made as soon as possible of the reason for taking a person's footwear impressions without consent. If force is used, a record shall be made of the circumstances and those present (Code D, para. 4.20).

Investigators' Manual, para. 1.8.5.1

20. Answer **A** — The doctrine of transferred *mens rea* is not restricted to offences under the Offences Against the Person Act 1861, making answer B incorrect. The issue of transferred *mens rea* can be important in relation to the liability of accessories. If the principal's intentions (MARTIN) are to be extended to an accessory (WEBBER), it must be shown that those intentions were either contemplated and accepted by that person at the time of the offence, or that they were 'transferred'. So transferred *mens rea* is applicable to accessories and answer D is incorrect. An example is provided in the *Blackstone's Police Investigators' Manual* where a person (X) encourages another (Y) to assault Z. Y decides to attack a different person instead. X will not be liable for that assault because it was not contemplated or agreed by X. If, however, in trying to assault Z, Y happens to injure a third person inadvertently, then 'transferred *mens rea*' may result in X being liable for those injuries even though X had no wish for that person to be so injured. In trying to cause criminal damage to ASHCROFT's car, MARTIN damages a car owned by GOODEY—WEBBER would be liable for that damage but

would not be liable for the assault as that was not contemplated by WEBBER so answer A is correct and answer C is incorrect.

Investigators' Manual, para. 1.2.11

21. Answer **A** — Answer D is incorrect as for the power under s. 32 to be lawfully used, the officer would have to have reasonable grounds for believing (not suspecting) that the arrested person may present a danger to themselves or others. Answer B is incorrect as the officer has a power under s. 32(2)(ii) to search the arrested person for anything which might be evidence relating to *an offence* (not just the offence for which the person was arrested). Answer C is incorrect as PC DEARLOVE can search in NEDD's mouth (see s. 32(4)). Answer A is the correct answer as trespassing on land with a firearm is a *summary only* offence. Section 32(2)(b) allows an officer to enter and search any premises where the offender was when arrested or immediately before for evidence relating to the offence but only if the offence for which he/she was arrested was *indictable*.

Investigators' Manual, para. 1.6.7

22. Answer **A** — A significant statement is one which appears capable of being used in evidence against the suspect, in particular a direct admission of guilt (Code C, para. 11.4A) and must have been made in the presence and hearing of a police officer (or other police staff member) (Code C, para. 11.4)—it could be made at any location (answer B is incorrect). Answer D is incorrect as a 'significant statement' will be made prior to a caution not after it. The suspect must be given the opportunity to clarify, confirm, deny or add to an earlier statement—the statement should be put to the suspect at the beginning of the interview, after caution and before questioning (answer C is incorrect).

Investigators' Manual, para. 1.9.3

23. Answer **C** — Section 3A(4) of the Bail Act 1976 states that where a custody officer has granted bail in criminal proceedings, he/she or *another custody officer* serving at the *same police station* may, at the request of the person to whom it was granted, vary the conditions of bail and in doing so he/she may impose conditions or more serious conditions, making answers A, B and D incorrect.

Investigators' Manual, para. 1.10.7.3

24. Answer **B** — Where a person is remanded in custody, it normally means detention in prison. However, s. 128 of the Magistrates' Courts Act 1980 provides that a magistrates' court may commit them to detention at a police station:

- for a period not exceeding three clear days (24 hours for persons under 18 (s. 91(5) of the Legal Aid, Sentencing and Punishment of Offenders Act 2012) (s. 128(7));
- for the purpose of enquiries into offences (other than the offence for which he/she appears before the court) (s. 128(8)(a));
- as soon as the need ceases, he/she must be brought back before the magistrates (s. 128(8)(b));
- the conditions of detention and periodic review apply as if the person was arrested without warrant on suspicion of having committed an offence (s. 128(8)(c) and (d)).

So GIBB could be remanded in police custody for a period not exceeding three clear days and MUTCH could be remanded in police custody for a period not exceeding 24 hours, meaning that answers A, C and D are incorrect.

Investigators' Manual, para. 1.10.10

25. Answer **A** — The relevant rank of an authorising officer for a CHIS is a superintendent and above. However, in urgent cases where it is not reasonably practicable to have the application considered by someone of that rank in the same organisation, an inspector may generally give the relevant authorisation (making answers C and D incorrect). Unless it is renewed, the authorisation given by a superintendent will ordinarily cease to have effect after 12 months, beginning on the day it was granted (Regulation of Investigatory Powers Act 2000, s. 43(3)(b)). If that authorisation was given orally by a superintendent in an urgent case, it will only last for 72 hours unless renewed and, where the case is urgent and the authority was given by an inspector, it will cease to have effect 72 hours later unless renewed (s. 43(3)(a)), making answer B incorrect. An authorisation by an inspector must be in writing.

Investigators' Manual, para. 1.12.3

26. Answer **C** — The Bail Act 1976, s. 6 creates two offences in relation to absconding and states:

(1) If a person who has been released on bail in criminal proceedings fails without reasonable cause to surrender to custody he shall be guilty of an offence.
(2) If a person who—
  (a) has been released on bail in criminal proceedings, and
  (b) having reasonable cause therefor, has failed to surrender to custody,
  fails to surrender to custody at the appointed place as soon after the appointed time as is reasonably practicable he shall be guilty of an offence.

Answer B is incorrect as s. 6 applies where:

- the police grant bail to a suspect to appear at the police station;
- the police grant bail to a defendant to appear at court on the first appearance;
- the court grants bail to the defendant to return to court at a later date.

Answer B is further incorrect as in *Laidlaw* v *Atkinson* (1986) The Times, 2 August, it was held that being mistaken about the day on which one should have appeared was not a reasonable excuse. Answer D is incorrect as failure to give to a person granted bail in criminal proceedings a copy of the record of the decision does not constitute reasonable cause for that person's failure to surrender to custody (s. 6(4)). As these are not 'reasonable excuses', this makes answer C correct.

Investigators' Manual, para. 1.10.9

27. Answer **B** — Group identifications may take place either with the suspect's consent and cooperation or covertly without their consent, making answer A incorrect. Answer C is incorrect as group identifications can involve stationary or moving groups. If it is practicable, then the group identification process will be video recorded but this might not be possible (making answer D incorrect). Group identifications should only take place in police stations for reasons of safety, security or because it is not practicable to hold them elsewhere (correct answer B).

Investigators' Manual, para. 1.8.10

28. Answer **B** — Answer C is incorrect as whilst it is true that 'but for' KINGSLEY's actions NORTH would not be dead, that liability is not associated with a rule that states that the chain of causation cannot be broken—in fact, it can be broken and there are numerous examples of that in the 'Intervening Act' section of the *Blackstone's Police Investigators' Manual*. Answer B is correct as KINGSLEY is liable for the death of NORTH because of the rule that says defendants must 'take their victims as they find them'. This means that if victims have a particular characteristic, such as a very thin skull or a very nervous disposition, which makes the consequences of an act against them much more acute, that is the defendant's bad luck. An example of this principle can be seen in *R* v *Harvey* [2010] EWCA Crim 1317 where, during a 'domestic tiff', the offender threw a television remote control at his wife, which hit her behind the ear. Unknown to anyone, she had an unusual weakness of the vertebral artery, which ruptured and caused her death. Save for the death, the offence charged would have been one of battery. Such characteristics (e.g. where an assault victim died after refusing a blood transfusion on religious grounds (*R* v *Blaue* [1975] 1 WLR 1411)) will not break the causal link—this makes answers A and D incorrect.

Investigators' Manual, para. 1.3.7

29. Answer **C** — Code B, para. 3.4 states that applications for all search warrants must be made with the written authority of an officer of at least the rank of *inspector* (although in urgent cases where such an officer is not readily available, the most senior officer on duty may authorise the application), making answer A incorrect. Answer B is incorrect as s. 16(3) of PACE states that entry and search under such a warrant must be made within *three* months from the date of its issue. If the warrant is an all premises warrant, no premises which are not specified in it may be entered and searched unless a police officer of at least the rank of *inspector* has, in writing, authorised them to be entered (s. 16(3A)) making answer D incorrect.

Investigators' Manual, para. 1.6.4

30. Answer **D** — The Police and Criminal Evidence Act 1984, s. 18(1) states:

    A constable may enter and search any premises *occupied or controlled* by a person who is under arrest for an indictable offence, if he has reasonable grounds for suspecting that there is on the premises evidence, other than items subject to legal privilege that relates—

    (a) to that offence; or
    (b) to some other indictable offence which is connected with or similar to that offence.

    'Occupied or controlled' is highlighted as many persons believe that it states 'owns'.

    Reasonable suspicion that someone occupies or controls premises is not sufficient, making D the correct option.

Investigators' Manual, para. 1.6.7

31. Answer **A** — When a man calls another man 'mate' or 'lad', it is not demeaning. However, using words like 'chick, babes, bobs, honey, hun and sweetie' are all demeaning and infantilising ways of referring to women (*Hartley* v *D Hollowell & Sons Ltd* [2021] UKET Case No. 2405802/2020).

Investigators' Manual, para. 1.1.4.8

32. Answer **D** — There is no liability for a failure (or omission) to act unless the law specifically imposes a DUTY on a person. That DUTY can arise from a number of circumstances, the main ones being:

D Dangerous situation created by the defendant. For example, in *R* v *Miller* [1983] 2 AC 161 the defendant was 'sleeping rough' and entered a building and fell asleep on a mattress while smoking a cigarette. When he awoke, he saw the mattress was smouldering but instead of calling for help or doing anything about the smouldering mattress, he simply moved into another room in the building and fell asleep. The mattress caught fire and the fire spread to the rest of the building. The defendant was convicted of arson, not for starting the fire but for failing to do anything about it.

U Under statute, contract or a person's public 'office'. Examples would include:

- Statute—a driver who is involved in a damage or injury accident fails to stop at the scene of the accident (s. 170 of the Road Traffic Act 1988), a driver who fails to cooperate with a preliminary test procedure (s. 6(6) of the Road Traffic Act 1988) or a person who does not disclose information in relation to terrorism (s. 19 of the Terrorism Act 2000).
- Contract—a crossing keeper omitted to close the gates (a job that was part of his contractual obligations) at a level crossing and a person was subsequently killed by a passing train (*R* v *Pittwood* (1902) 19 TLR 37).
- Public office—whilst on duty, a police officer stood aside and watched as a man was beaten to death outside a nightclub. The officer then left the scene, without calling for assistance or summoning an ambulance. For this, the officer was convicted of the common law offence of misconduct in a public office (*R* v *Dytham* [1979] QB 722).

T Taken it upon him/herself—the defendant voluntarily undertakes to care for another who is unable to care for him/herself as a result of age, illness or infirmity and then fails to care for that person. For example, in *R* v *Stone* [1977] QB 354 the defendant accepted a duty to care for her partner's mentally ill sister who subsequently died from neglect.

Y Young person—in circumstances where the defendant is in a parental relationship with a child or a young person, i.e. an obligation exists for the parent to look after the health and welfare of the child and he/she does not do so.

Answers A and B are incorrect as whilst there is no statutory obligation/parental relationship between Lance DALLOW and his partner TITUS/brother Brian, the 'T' of the mnemonic clearly creates such a liability—that is, for both persons (making answer C incorrect).

Investigators' Manual, para. 1.3.5

33. Answer **B** — Section 21A of the Criminal Procedure and Investigations Act 1996 introduced a Code of Practice for Arranging and Conducting Interviews of Witnesses Notified by the Accused. The Code sets out guidance that police officers and other persons charged with investigating offences must follow if they arrange or conduct interviews of proposed witnesses whose details are disclosed to the prosecution under the 1996 Act. If an investigator wishes to interview a witness, the witness must be asked whether they consent to being interviewed and informed that an interview is being requested following their identification by the accused as a proposed witness under s. 6A(2) or s. 6C of the Act and that they are not obliged to attend the proposed interview (correct answer B). The witness should be informed that they are entitled to be accompanied by a solicitor at the interview (making answer A incorrect) but nothing in this Code of Practice creates any duty on the part of the Legal Services Commission

to provide funding for any such attendance (making answer C incorrect). Answer D is incorrect as there is no requirement for the interviewing officer to be of any specific rank.

Investigators' Manual, para. 1.11.11.7

34. Answer **A** — If an authorising officer, of superintendent rank or above, considers that access to a solicitor will interfere with evidence relating to an indictable offence, then access to that solicitor may be delayed, making answer D incorrect. This authorisation to delay access is not a 'blanket' authorisation to deny access to all legal advisers and in the example given in the question, the authorising officer should consider offering the detained person access to another solicitor on the Duty Solicitor scheme, making answer C incorrect. The consultation with a solicitor must be in private (Code C, para. 6.1). In *Brennan* v *United Kingdom* (2001) 34 EHRR 507, the court held that a suspect's right to communicate confidentially with a solicitor 'is part of the basic requirements of a fair trial'. The court found that there had been a breach of Article 6(3)(c) because a police officer had been present during a suspect's first interview with his solicitor, making answer B incorrect.

Investigators' Manual, paras 1.7.11, 1.7.23

35. Answer **A** — The Police and Criminal Evidence Act 1984, s. 80 states:

(2A) In any proceedings the spouse or civil partner of a person charged in the proceedings shall, subject to subsection (4) below, be compellable—
  (a) to give evidence on behalf of any other person charged in the proceedings but only in respect of any specified offence with which that other person is charged; or
  (b) to give evidence for the *prosecution* but only in respect of any *specified offence* with which any person is charged in the proceedings.

(3) In relation to the spouse or civil partner of a person charged in any proceedings, an offence is a specified offence for the purposes of subsection (2A) above if—
  (a) it involves an assault on, or injury or a threat of injury to, the spouse or civil partner or a person who was at the material time under the age of 16;
  (b) it is a sexual offence alleged to have been committed in respect of a person who was at the material time under that age; or
  (c) it consists of attempting or conspiring to commit, or of aiding, abetting, counselling, procuring or inciting the commission of, an offence falling within paragraph (a) or (b) above.

The law in s. 80(2A) means that answer D is incorrect as a wife can be a compellable witness against her husband in relation to certain offences. Answer C is incorrect as the offence of murder in not contained in s. 80(3). In this situation, Emma RAILTON would not be a compellable witness. However, there is no requirement to tell a wife that she is not a compellable witness against her husband before interviewing her about a crime of which her husband is suspected (answer B is incorrect). A statement obtained from the wife in such circumstances could be admitted in evidence even though the wife refused to give evidence against her husband, provided it did not lead to an injustice (*R* v *L* [2008] EWCA Crim 973) (correct answer A).

Investigators' Manual, para. 1.5.8.5

36. Answer **B** — Section 16 of the Offences Against the Person Act 1861 states that a person who, without lawful excuse, makes to another a threat, intending that the other will fear that it will be carried out, to kill that other or a third person shall be guilty of an offence. The fact that CHURCH does not believe the threat is immaterial (making answer A incorrect). It can be committed via delivery of the threat to a third party (making answer C incorrect). It does not matter that the threat is made to kill at some time in the future—it is the intention to create the fear in the mind of another that is all important (making answer D incorrect).

Investigators' Manual, para. 2.7.8

37. Answer **D** — The Public Order Act 1986, s. 18 states:

(1) A person who uses threatening, abusive or insulting words or behaviour, or displays any written material which is threatening, abusive or insulting, is guilty of an offence if—
   (a) he intends thereby to stir up racial hatred, or
   (b) having regard to all the circumstances racial hatred is likely to be stirred up thereby.

(2) An offence under this section may be committed in a public or a private place, except that no offence is committed where the words or behaviour are used, or the written material is displayed, by a person inside a dwelling and are not heard or seen except by other persons in that or another dwelling [correct answer D].

Section 18(2) provides an exception to the offence, setting out circumstances where the offence *will not* be committed—this is the situation with HOPPER—he *has not* committed the offence (answers A and C are incorrect). Answer B is incorrect as it can be committed by someone in a dwelling if the activity was heard or seen by a person who was not in the same dwelling or another one; for example, if a person walking on the street heard HOPPER's language then the offence could be committed.

Investigators' Manual, para. 2.8.2.1

38. Answer **C** — Special defences are only available in relation to a charge of murder so the defence could never be used in respect of a charge of attempted murder (ruling out answer B). Answer D is incorrect as s. 54(2) of the Coroners and Justice Act 2009 states that whether a loss of control is sudden or not will not impact on the availability of the defence. A 'loss of control' must have a qualifying trigger (s. 54(1)(b) of the Coroners and Justice Act 2009). In determining whether a loss of control had a qualifying trigger, the fact that a thing done or said constituted sexual infidelity is to be disregarded (s. 55(6)), meaning that answer A is incorrect and making answer C correct in the process.

Investigators' Manual, para. 2.1.3.2

39. Answer **A** — Nobody is saying that CLARKE is guilty of an offence at this stage—this question simply asks 'Is he in possession of the cocaine?' and the answer is 'Yes' (answer A) because possession is a neutral concept, not implying any fault, blame or guilt. To be in 'possession' of something, the person needs to have custody/control of it and to know that the thing in question is under his/her control (making answer C incorrect). CLARKE knows he has custody/control over the envelope so he possesses it. It does not matter that he thinks it contains £200 cash or that he did not know that it contained cocaine (answers B and D)—he knew it contained something so he is therefore in possession of that something.

Investigators' Manual, paras 2.2.3 to 2.2.3.7

damage had occurred and spoke to the defendant who was, by that time, sitting in his own house. The defendant made comments demonstrating hostility based on the victim's membership of a racial group. The defendant was convicted of racially aggravated criminal damage but appealed and the conviction was quashed. The court held that the wording of the statute meant that any hostility had to be demonstrated *immediately* before or *immediately* after the substantive offence and that the courts below (magistrates') had not been entitled to consider the retrospective effect of the comments made later by the defendant (correct answer A).

Investigators' Manual, paras 2.6.2 to 2.6.3.2

45. Answer **D** — Section 1 of the Road Traffic Act 1988 states that a person who causes the death of another person by driving a mechanically propelled vehicle dangerously on a road or other public place is guilty of an offence. As the incident occurred on private land, the offence has not been committed (correct answer D). This immediately makes answers A and C incorrect as they are 'Yes' options but, in addition, answer A is incorrect as the fact that a driver was adversely affected by alcohol is a circumstance relevant to the issue of dangerous driving, but *is not* in itself determinative to prove the offence (*R* v *Webster* [2006] 2 Cr App R 103). Answer C is incorrect as stated, however it is relevant to point out that where the defendant is charged under s. 1, evidence of drink will be admissible where the quantity of it may have adversely affected the quality of the person's driving (*R* v *Woodward* [1995] RTR 130). Answer B states that the reason the offence has not been committed is that the death did not occur *while* LAMBERT was driving but this is incorrect as the Court of Appeal has clarified that this offence relates to causing death *by* driving and not causing death *while* driving and therefore the 'driving' does not have to be coextensive with the collision that resulted in the death. In *R* v *Jenkins* [2012] EWCA Crim 2909, the court held that parking a van to make a delivery, leaving it in conditions of poor visibility where another vehicle collided with it, was certainly a causal link to the fatality that occurred.

Investigators' Manual, para. 2.14.5

46. Answer **C** — Section 17(2) states that if a person, at the time of his committing or being arrested for an offence specified in sch. 1 to this Act, has in his possession a firearm or imitation firearm, he shall be guilty of an offence under this subsection unless he shows that he had it in his possession for a lawful object. The offence applies to firearms and imitation firearms (so both the rifle and the imitation revolver would be covered), meaning that answer A is incorrect. Child abduction under s. 2 of the Child Abduction Act 1984 is a sch. 1 offence, meaning that answer B is incorrect. It does not matter whether the person concerned is ultimately found guilty of the offence for which they were arrested, making answer D incorrect.

Investigators' Manual, para. 2.3.9.5

47. Answer **D** — 'Explosive substance' includes any materials for making any explosive substance; any implement or apparatus used, or intended or adapted to be used, for causing or aiding any explosion (s. 9(1)). The definition of 'explosive' under the Explosives Act 1875 also applies to this offence (*R* v *Wheatley* [1979] 1 WLR 144). Therefore fireworks and petrol bombs will be

covered (*R* v *Bouch* [1983] QB 246). This means that answer A is incorrect. The Explosive Substances Act 1883, s. 4 states:

(1) Any person who makes or knowingly has in his possession or under his control any explosive substance under such circumstances as to give rise to a reasonable suspicion that he is not making it or does not have it in his possession or under his control for a lawful object, shall, unless he can show that he made it or had it in his possession or under his control for a lawful object, be guilty of [an offence] ...

The 'explosive substance' does not have to be made or possessed to cause injury only—it is about making or having it under your possession or control for a lawful object, making answer C incorrect. As the offence is about making, possession or control, DEVINE and SURTEES commit the offence (correct answer D), making answer B incorrect.

Investigators' Manual, para. 2.4.8

48. Answer **C** — As this is an offence of intent, there is no need for a result to take place before the offence is complete, making answer D incorrect. Answer A is incorrect as the offence can be carried out for the benefit of anyone, including the person making the unauthorised access. The offences to which this offence applies are defined under s. 2(2) of the Act; KENDALL's activities *do not* constitute such an offence (making answer B incorrect). This is because he intends to steal *information* and this cannot be stolen as it is not property (*Oxford* v *Moss* (1978) 68 Cr App R 183) (see *Theft*, para. 3.1.7).

Investigators' Manual, para. 2.5.2.3

49. Answer **D** — Under s. 89(2) of the Police Act 1996, it is an offence to *wilfully* obstruct a police officer or any person assisting the officer in the lawful execution of his/her duty (not accidentally—answer C is incorrect). It does not require an intentional or reckless element (answer A is incorrect). Answer B is incorrect as although obstruction can be committed by an omission to do something, that is only where a person was already obliged to undertake some duty for a police officer (and GANGAR would have no such obligation in this situation). The obstruction must be wilful—GANGAR may have accidentally made it harder for the officer to carry out his duty but that would not mean that he commits this offence.

Investigators' Manual, para. 2.7.7.3

50. Answer **A** — The Misuse of Drugs Act 1971, s. 19 states that it is an offence for a person to incite another to commit an offence under any other provision of the Act. Answers C and D are incorrect as a person inciting an undercover police officer may commit an offence under s. 19, even though there was no possibility of the officer actually being induced to commit the offence (*DPP* v *Armstrong* [2000] Crim LR 379). When BARBER asks the officer to sell him drugs, he 'incites' the officer to 'supply a controlled drug' (an offence under s. 4(3) of the Act (correct answer A as the question asks at what point an offence is 'first' committed)).

Investigators' Manual, para. 2.2.13

51. Answer **A** — Only one criminal damage offence is capable of being racially and/or religiously aggravated ('simple' criminal damage—Criminal Damage Act 1971, s. 1(1)) meaning that answer C is incorrect. Section 28 of the Crime and Disorder Act 1998 states:

> (1) An offence is racially or religiously aggravated for the purposes of sections 29 to 32 . . . if—
> (a) at the time of committing the offence, or immediately before or after doing so, the offender demonstrates towards the victim of the offence hostility based on the victim's membership (or presumed membership) of a racial or religious group; or
> (b) the offence is *motivated (wholly or partly) by hostility* towards members of a racial or religious group based on their membership of that group.

As the offence was motivated by religious hostility, answer D is incorrect. A 'presumption' of racial/religious identity may well be wrong—that does not matter, so the fact that ROSE is not from the religious group BOTTING presumed him to be does not stop the offence being committed therefore answer B is incorrect.

Investigators' Manual, paras 2.6.2 to 2.6.3.7

52. Answer **B** — The Public Order Act 1986, s. 29B states:

> (1) A person who uses threatening words or behaviour, or displays any written material which is threatening, is guilty of an offence if he intends thereby to stir up religious hatred or hatred on the grounds of sexual orientation.
> (2) An offence under this section is committed in a public or private place, except that no offence is committed where the words or behaviour are used, or the written material is displayed, by a person inside a dwelling and are not heard or seen except by other persons in that or another dwelling.

In proceedings for an offence under this section, it is a defence for the accused to prove that he/she was inside a dwelling and that he/she had no reason to believe that the words or behaviour used, or the written material displayed, would be heard or seen by a person outside that or any other dwelling.

These circumstances do not amount to an offence (correct answer B)—s. 29B(2) states that 'no offence is committed' when the written material is displayed by a person inside a dwelling (GARCIA) and not seen except by other persons in that or another dwelling (AKERMAN). This means that answers A and C are incorrect—no offence has been committed. Answer D is incorrect as even if GARCIA did intend to stir up religious hatred by displaying the flag, s. 29B(2) means that no offence is committed.

Investigators' Manual, para. 2.8.2.5

53. Answer **D** — Affray can take place in public or in private (making answer A incorrect). The offence does not require two or more persons to use or threaten to use unlawful violence (making answer B incorrect). Answer C is incorrect as affray can be committed by using or threatening to use unlawful violence. The House of Lords held that in order to prove the offence of affray, the threat of unlawful violence has to be towards a person(s) present at the scene (*I* v *DPP* [2001] UKHL 10). Once this element has been proved, it will be necessary to prove the second element; namely, whether the defendant's conduct would have caused a hypothetical person present at the scene to fear for his/her personal safety (*R* v *Sanchez* (1996)

160 JP 321 and *R* v *Carey* [2006] EWCA Crim 17). However, where the likelihood of a hypothetical person of reasonable firmness being present was low, this element of the offence was not satisfied. In *R (On the Application of Leeson)* v *DPP* [2010] EWHC 994 (Admin), a woman had issued a drunken threat to kill her long-term partner while holding a knife, in a bathroom in an otherwise unoccupied house. In these circumstances, the court held that there was no possibility of hypothetical bystanders fearing for their safety.

Investigators' Manual, para. 2.13.2

54. Answer **A** — Section 34(1) of the Policing and Crime Act 2009 states that a court may grant an injunction against a respondent aged 14 or over (making answer A correct). If an injunction is granted it will be because two conditions are met, the first being that the court is satisfied *on the balance of probabilities* that the respondent has engaged in or has encouraged or assisted gang-related violence, or gang-related drug-dealing activity (rather than beyond all reasonable doubt (incorrect answer B)). Section 34(5) states that for the purposes of this section, something is 'gang-related' if it occurs in the course of, or is otherwise related to, the activities of a group that consists of at least three (not five—incorrect answer C) people, and has one or more characteristics that enable its members to be identified by others as a group. The court *may* attach a power of arrest in relation to any prohibition in the injunction or any requirement in the injunction *other than* one which has the effect of requiring the respondent to participate in particular activities (s. 36) (incorrect answer D).

Investigators' Manual, para. 2.12.2

55. Answer **C** — The Theft Act 1968, s. 21 states:

(1) A person is guilty of blackmail if, with a view to gain for himself or another or with intent to cause loss to another, he makes any unwarranted demand with menaces; and for this purpose a demand with menaces is unwarranted unless the person making it does so in the belief—
(a) that he has reasonable grounds for making the demand; and
(b) that the use of the menaces is a proper means of reinforcing the demand.

The Court of Appeal has held that words or conduct which would not intimidate or influence anyone to respond to the demand would not be 'menaces'. As such, the term requires threats and conduct of such a nature and extent that a person of normal stability and courage might be influenced or made apprehensive so as to give in to the demands (*R* v *Clear* [1968] 1 QB 670).

Menaces will therefore include threats but these must be significant *to the victim*. If a threat bears a particular significance for a victim (such as being locked in the boot of a car to someone who is claustrophobic), that will be enough provided the defendant was aware of that fact. If a victim is particularly timid and the defendant knows it, that timidity may be taken into account when assessing whether or not the defendant's conduct was 'menacing' (*R* v *Garwood* [1987] 1 WLR 319). So the menaces directed towards NICKLIN and JAKEMAN would be relevant and as the offence is complete at the moment the demand is made, WALKER commits the offence (answer C, making answers A, B and D incorrect).

Investigators' Manual, paras 3.3.1 to 3.3.3

56. Answer **A** — Section 3 of the Criminal Damage Act 1971 states that a person who has anything in his custody or under his control intending without lawful excuse to use it or cause or permit another to use it (a) to destroy or damage any property belonging to some other person; or (b) to destroy or damage his own or the user's property in a way which he knows is likely to endanger the life of some other person shall be guilty of an offence. This offence covers anything which a defendant has 'in his custody or under his control', a broader term than 'possession', making answer B incorrect. Answer C is incorrect as the offence does not require the intention to endanger a person's life (although it can be committed in that way). There is a statutory power to apply to a magistrate for a search warrant under s. 6 of the Criminal Damage Act 1971 for anything that could be used or is intended to be used to destroy or damage property.

The Criminal Damage Act 1971, s. 6 states:

(1) If it is made to appear by information on oath before a justice of the peace that there is reasonable cause to believe that any person has in his custody or under his control or on his premises anything which there is reasonable cause to believe has been used or is intended for use without lawful excuse—
  (a) to destroy or damage property belonging to another; or
  (b) to destroy or damage any property in a way likely to endanger the life of another, the justice may grant a warrant authorising any constable to search for and seize that thing.

So a warrant could be obtained to search for the brake fluid, making answer A correct and answer D incorrect.

Investigators' Manual, para. 3.9.6

57. Answer **B** — Any representation made must be one as to fact or law, so a broken promise is not in itself a false representation. However, a statement may be false if it misrepresents the current intentions or state of mind of the person making it or anyone else. This MCQ is a good example of such behaviour. HILLIER visits PEACH's house and tells PEACH that he needs emergency work carried out on his roof. HILLIER states that he is in a position to do the work immediately but only if PEACH pays him £150 there and then. PEACH gives HILLIER the money and HILLIER then leaves without carrying out the work; the truth of the matter is that HILLIER had never intended to carry out the work. Such a 'promise' by HILLIER would amount to an offence as it involved a false representation, i.e. he never intended to keep the promise (this makes answer A incorrect). Answer D is incorrect as the offence is complete the moment the false representation is made. Answer C is incorrect as the mode of trial for the fraud offence is not related to the value of the goods concerned (in a way that you might associate with low-value shoplifting).

Investigators' Manual, paras 3.7.2 to 3.7.4

58. Answer **B** — There are two forms of burglary—s. 9(1)(a) and s. 9(1)(b). The Theft Act 1968, s. 9 states:

(1) A person is guilty of burglary if—
  (a) he enters any building or part of a building as a trespasser and with intent to commit any such offence as is mentioned in subsection (2) below; or ...

(2) The offences referred to in subsection (1)(a) above are offences of stealing anything in the building or part of a building in question, of inflicting on any person therein any grievous bodily harm and of doing unlawful damage to the building or anything therein.

The s. 9(1)(a) offence is committed at one point only—the point of entry. The necessary intention must be in the mind of the defendant at that time and at no stage does XAVIER ever 'enter' with intent so there is no offence under s. 9(1)(a) to consider at any stage.

The Theft Act 1968, s. 9 states:

(1) A person is guilty of burglary if—
   (b) having entered any building or part of a building as a trespasser he steals or attempts to steal anything in the building or that part of it or inflicts or attempts to inflict on any person therein any grievous bodily harm.

XAVIER has entered the warehouse as a trespasser when he breaks in looking for shelter but when he turns on the electric fire to warm himself up this is not 'stealing' as electricity is not 'property' for the purposes of the offence of theft, so no burglary is committed at point A. However, when he steals the £30 cash he does commit a s. 9(1)(b) offence (answer B is the correct answer as the question asks when a burglary is first committed). There is no burglary at point C (this is criminal damage)—a further burglary under s. 9(1)(b) is committed when XAVIER steals the batteries (point D).

Investigators' Manual, paras 3.4.1 to 3.4.5

59. Answer **D** — The Fraud Act 2006, s. 6 states:

(1) A person is guilty of an offence if he has in his possession or under his control any article for use in the course of or in connection with any fraud.

An 'article' can be anything whatsoever. For the purposes of ss. 6 and 7 of the Act, an 'article' includes any program or data held in electronic form. Examples of cases where electronic programs or data could be used in fraud are:

- a computer program that generates credit card numbers;
- a computer template that can be used for producing blank utility bills;
- a computer file that contains lists of other people's credit card details.

So the computer program and the template found on EISEMAN's computer are 'articles' for the purposes of s. 6. The offence under s. 6 can be committed anywhere at all, including the home of the defendant (making answer B incorrect). It is committed when the defendant has articles in his/her possession and also when the defendant has them in his/her control, so the defendant may be some distance away from the articles and still commit the offence. The s. 6 offence applies to 'any fraud' which will therefore include all fraud offences under the 2006 Act. However, answers A and C are incorrect and answer D is the correct answer as the offence is only committed in respect of *future offences* and not offences that have already taken place (*R* v *Sakalauskas* [2014] 1 All ER 1231).

Investigators' Manual, para. 3.7.7

60. Answer **A** — Section 27 of the Theft Act 1968 allows for the admissibility of previous misconduct and states:

> (3) Where a person is being proceeded against for handling stolen goods (but not for any offence other than handling stolen goods), then at any stage of the proceedings, if evidence has been given of his having or arranging to have in his possession the goods the subject of the charge, or of his undertaking or assisting in, or arranging to undertake or assist in, their retention, removal, disposal or realisation, the following evidence shall be admissible for the purpose of proving that he knew or believed the goods to be stolen goods—
> (a) evidence that he has had in his possession, or has undertaken or assisted in the retention, removal, disposal or realisation of, stolen goods from any theft taking place not earlier than 12 months before the offence charged; and
> (b) (provided that seven days' notice in writing has been given to him of the intention to prove the conviction) evidence that he has within the five years preceding the date of the offence charged been convicted of theft or of handling stolen goods.

Therefore SHACKLOCK's previous conviction and the evidence that he had stolen property in his possession nine months before the handling offence he is charged with are admissible, making answers B, C and D incorrect.

Investigators' Manual, para. 3.6.6

61. Answer **C** — Robbery is committed when a person steals and immediately before or at the time of doing so, and in order to do so, they use force on any person or put or seek to put any person in fear of being then and there subjected to force. What this means is that when force is threatened the person being threatened must fear force for *him/herself and not for another*. So when the gun is pointed towards the back of the customer, the cashier cannot fear force on the customer's behalf meaning that at points A and B no offence of robbery has been committed.

When force is used, it can be used on *anyone* in order to commit the theft. So when WRIGHT hits the customer, force is being used on *any person* in order to commit a theft. When the cashier hands over the money, at that point the offence of robbery is complete, making answer D incorrect.

Investigators' Manual, para. 3.2.1

62. Answer **D** — Under s. 4(2) of the Theft Act 1968, you cannot generally steal land; however, there are exceptions to this rule. Things growing wild on any land (in this case, the raspberries growing on land belonging to STEBBING) are 'property' and could be stolen by a person not in possession of the land (DOWNING) if he/she severed and appropriated them. However, s. 4(3) of the Act tells us that a person who picks mushrooms, flowers, fruit and foliage growing wild on any land will not commit theft by so doing unless the picking is done for reward, sale or other commercial purpose; therefore, DOWNING does not commit theft in relation to the raspberries making answers A and C incorrect. Section 4(2)(c) states that theft can be committed by a tenant when that tenant appropriates the whole or part of any fixture or structure let to be used with the land. Examples of 'fixtures' would be a fireplace or a kitchen sink; a structure might be a greenhouse or a garden shed which is fixed to the land. A tenant

cannot steal land such as topsoil or a lilac tree growing in the garden of the rented premises as these things are not 'fixtures or structures', making answer B incorrect.

Investigators' Manual, para. 3.1.5

63. Answer **C** — To commit a s. 9(1)(a) burglary, the offender must enter a building or part of a building as a trespasser with the intention of stealing anything therein, committing grievous bodily harm or criminal damage—GRIMSHAW had none of these intentions so a s. 9(1)(a) offence is not committed, making answer A incorrect. Answer B is incorrect as an aggravated burglary is an aggravated version of the s. 9(1)(a) offence or the s. 9(1)(b) offence. We have established that GRIMSHAW has not committed a s. 9(1)(a) offence and that remains the case when he enters the living room. As a s. 9(1)(a) can only be committed at the point of entry, no aggravated s. 9(1)(a) has been committed. Inside the living room, he can only commit a s. 9(1)(b) burglary—having entered a building or part of a building as a trespasser, he steals or attempts to steal, commits or attempts to commit grievous bodily harm. He has not done anything that fits the s. 9(1)(b) offence so when he picks up the poker, this is not a burglary. However, when he picks up the poker he decides to use it to cause grievous bodily harm and at that stage the poker becomes a weapon of offence (instant arming). When he moves from the living room into the hallway, he enters part of a building (the hallway) as a trespasser and at that stage he intends to cause BAGBY grievous bodily harm—this is a s. 9(1)(a) burglary. At the time of the s. 9(1)(a), he has with him a weapon of offence and consequently commits an aggravated burglary at that stage (answer C) making answer D incorrect.

Investigators' Manual, paras 3.4.1 to 3.5.1

64. Answer **A** — Robbery is committed when a person steals and, immediately before or at the time of doing so and in order to do so, they use force on any person or put or seek to put any person in fear of being then and there subjected to force. However, there must be a theft for a robbery to occur ('and thief and steal shall be construed accordingly'). If there is no theft, then there is no robbery. Here there is no theft because CREED honestly believes that he has a lawful right to deprive TINSLEY of the property. The circumstances of the question are very similar to the case of *R* v *Robinson* [1977] Crim LR 173, where D, who was owed £7 by P's wife, approached P, brandishing a knife. A fight followed, during which P dropped a £5 note. D picked it up and demanded the remaining £2 owed to him. Allowing D's appeal against a conviction for robbery, the Court of Appeal held that the prosecution had to prove that D was guilty of theft, and that he would not be (under s. 2(1)(a) of the Theft Act 1968) if he believed that he had a right in law to deprive P of the money, even though he knew that he was not entitled to use the knife to get it, i.e. there was no dishonesty. The fact that CREED knows the means he is using are wrong does not alter the dishonesty element.

Investigators' Manual, para. 3.2.1

65. Answer **A** — The offence of aggravated burglary under s. 10 of the Theft Act is committed when a person commits a burglary (under s. 9(1)(a) or s. 9(1)(b)) and at the time has with him/her any firearm, imitation firearm, any weapon of offence or any explosive. A weapon of offence is any article made, adapted or intended to cause injury to another or to incapacitate another. A bayonet is a weapon of offence per se and the rope is a weapon of offence as McCARRON intends to use it to incapacitate a person. The phrase 'has with him' means

'immediate control of the item'. As McCARRON *knows* about the bayonet then he 'has it with him'. This means that HUGHES and McCARRON commit the offence in relation to the bayonet (answer D is incorrect) but only McCARRON in relation to the rope (making answers B and C incorrect and answer A correct).

Investigators' Manual, para. 3.5.1

66. Answer **D** — The Proceeds of Crime Act 2002, s. 340 states:

(2) Criminal conduct is conduct which—
  (a) constitutes an offence in any part of the United Kingdom, or
  (b) would constitute an offence in any part of the United Kingdom if it occurred there.

The burglary at the warehouse is certainly ''criminal conduct'

The Proceeds of Crime Act 2002, s. 340 states:

(3) Property is criminal property if—
  (a) it constitutes a person's benefit from criminal conduct or it represents such a benefit (in whole or in part and whether directly or indirectly) and,
  (b) the alleged offender knows or suspects that it constitutes or represents such a benefit.

This means that the stolen washing machines are 'criminal property'.

The offence under s. 329 is committed when a person:

(a) acquires criminal property;
(b) uses criminal property;
(c) has possession of criminal property.

A thief who uses or retains possession of property that he/she has just stolen (this being criminal property as defined in s. 340) must therefore be guilty of an offence under s. 329(1)(b) or (c)—so RANKINE commits the offence meaning that answers A and C are incorrect. This offence is committed where a person knows or suspects that the property which is acquired etc. constitutes or represents his/her own or another's benefit from criminal conduct meaning that MILFORD also commits the offence, making answer B incorrect and answer D correct.

Investigators' Manual, paras 3.8.2, 3.8.3, 3.8.6

67. Answer **B** — Rape is committed when a person (A) intentionally penetrates the vagina, anus or mouth of another person (B) with his penis and B does not consent to the penetration and A does not reasonably believe B consents. A central element to the offence is the absence of consent (s. 74 of the Act) which states that a person consents if he/she agrees by choice and has the freedom and capacity to make that choice. In this situation, 'true' consent has been given so the offence has not been committed. Section 75 of the Act enables a court to presume that the victim did not consent if evidence presented in court proves that the circumstances involved any of the following: use of or fear of immediate violence against that or another person; unlawful detention; unconsciousness; inability to communicate due to physical disability; and/or substances that are capable of stupefying or overpowering (such as drugs) were non-consensually administered. It also has to be proved that the defendant knew of these circumstances and that the defendant carried out the act in question. Purely because violence was not used or threatened would not mean that a person consented to the relevant activity (answer D is incorrect). NAYLOR may have lied about his wealth and the promise to

marry but those lies were not about the nature or purpose of the relevant act, so answers A and C are incorrect.

Investigators' Manual, paras 4.2.1 to 4.2.6

68. Answer **A** — Answer C is incorrect as a 'relevant sexual offence' means an offence under Part I of the Sexual Offences Act 2003 (virtually all regularly occurring sexual offences) including aiding, abetting, counselling or procuring such an offence (s. 62(2)). Answer B is incorrect as the offence could cover any situation from the theft of drugs or equipment to be used in the course of the sexual offence and going equipped for burglary, to the taking of a vehicle or even dangerous driving with the intention in each case of committing the further relevant sexual offence. Answer D is incorrect as if A does commit the intended offence, he/she could be charged with the substantive sexual offence in addition to this offence (correct answer A).

Investigators' Manual, para. 4.6.2

69. Answer **A** — The Sexual Offences Act 2003, s. 63 states:

(1) A person commits an offence if—
 (a) he is a trespasser on any premises,
 (b) he intends to commit a relevant sexual offence on the premises, and
 (c) he knows that, or is reckless as to whether, he is a trespasser.

The moment FLOYD enters the garden of his neighbour, he is a trespasser but the offence is not committed as a 'relevant sexual offence' means an offence under part I of the Sexual Offences Act (virtually all regularly occurring sexual offences) including aiding, abetting, counselling or procuring such an offence (s. 62(2)); however, it *does not extend* to other sexual offences under the Protection of Children Act 1978.

Investigators' Manual, para. 4.6.3

70. Answer **B** — The Sexual Offences Act 2003, s. 1 states:

(1) A person (A) commits an offence if—
 (a) he intentionally penetrates the vagina, anus or mouth of another person (B) with his penis,
 (b) B does not consent to the penetration, and
 (c) A does not reasonably believe that B consents.

A person consents if they agree by choice, and have the freedom and capacity to make that choice (s. 74 of the Act)—any consent given must be 'true' consent, not simply a *submission* induced by fear or fraud. Therefore, if the person does not have any real choice in the matter, or the choice is not a genuine exercise of free will, then he/she has not 'consented'. Obtaining consent by fear or force would not be 'true consent' but if consent has been obtained by other means it does not automatically mean that the person consented (answer C is incorrect). FOSTER did consent to having sexual intercourse with BROOK but her consent was given with the express condition that BROOK would wear a condom—he did put on a condom but then took it off and this would amount to an offence of rape (answer A is incorrect). The question is closely associated to the case law decision in *Assange* v *Sweden* [2011] EWHC 2489 (Admin). In this case, the Divisional Court considered the situation in which A knew that B (the complainant) would only

77. Answer **A** — The Sexual Offences Act 2003, s. 2 states:

(1) A person (A) commits an offence if—
  (a) he intentionally penetrates the vagina or anus of another person (B) with a part of his body or anything else,
  (b) the penetration is sexual,
  (c) B does not consent to the penetration, and
  (d) A does not reasonably believe that B consents.

The victim's vagina and/or anus was not penetrated by FARRELL and ALLEN so the offence under s. 2 has not been committed (correct answer A).

Investigators' Manual, para. 4.3.1

78. Answer **C** — The Sexual Offences Act 2003, s. 61 states:

(1) A person commits an offence if he intentionally administers a substance to, or causes a substance to be taken by, another person (B)—
  (a) knowing that B does not consent, and
  (b) with the intention of stupefying or overpowering B, so as to enable *any person* to engage in a sexual activity that involves B.

Section 61(b) rules out answer B as being the correct option (the substance is administered to enable *any person* to engage in sexual activity).

This offence is aimed at the use of 'date rape' drugs administered without the victim's knowledge or consent but would also cover the use of any other substance with the relevant intention. It would cover CURRIN spiking MAUNSELL's soft drink with alcohol where MAUNSELL did not know she was consuming alcohol (making answer A incorrect). This offence applies both when A him/herself administers the substance to B, and where A causes the substance to be taken by B, for example when A persuades a friend (C) to administer a substance to B, so that A can have sex with B because C knows B socially and can more easily slip the substance into B's drink than A (making BROWN and CURRIN guilty of the offence) so answer D is incorrect and answer C is correct.

Investigators' Manual, para. 4.6.1

79. Answer **D** — Answer D is correct as this is an offence of rape—this answer relates to the case law in *Assange* v *Sweden* [2011] EWHC 2489 (Admin). Here the Divisional Court considered the situation in which A knew B (the complainant) would only consent to sexual intercourse if he used a condom. The court rejected the view that the conclusive presumption in s. 76 of the Sexual Offences Act 2003 would apply and concluded that the issue of consent could be determined under s. 74 rather than s. 76, and stated that it would be open to a jury to hold that if B had made it clear that she would only consent to sexual intercourse if A used a condom, then there would be no consent if, without B's consent, A did not use a condom or removed or tore the condom. A's conduct in having sexual intercourse without a condom in circumstances where B had made it clear that she would only have sexual intercourse if A did use a condom, would therefore amount to an offence. Answers A, B and C are *not* offences of rape.

Investigators' Manual, paras 4.2.3 to 4.2.6

80. Answer **B** — The offences under s. 1 of the Protection of Children Act 1978 or s. 160 of the Criminal Justice Act 1988 relate to photographs and images of a 'child'. For the purposes of both Acts, a person will be a 'child' if it appears from the evidence as a whole that he/she was, at the material time, under the age of 18 (Protection of Children Act 1978, s. 2(3) and Criminal Justice Act 1988, s. 160(4)).

Investigators' Manual, paras 4.4.12.3 to 4.4.12.4